The Lord's Feasts

A Study of How the Old Testament Feasts Find Their Fulfillment in Jesus Christ

Debbie Pyle

WESTBOW
PRESS
A DIVISION OF THOMAS NELSON
& ZONDERVAN

WestBow Press books may be ordered through booksellers or by contacting:

WestBow Press
A Division of Thomas Nelson & Zondervan
1663 Liberty Drive
Bloomington, IN 47403
www.westbowpress.com
1 (866) 928-1240

ISBN: 978-1-4908-8676-3 (sc)
ISBN: 978-1-4908-8677-0 (e)

Print information available on the last page.

WestBow Press rev. date: 07/16/2015

From the Author

Over the past twenty years, the Lord has graciously provided me with a number of Bible study opportunities. I have participated in, even had the privilege of facilitating studies prepared by Beth Moore, Kay Arthur, Henry Blackaby and others. During these studies, questions were often asked concerning the feasts.

Anyone who studies through the Bible will notice that the feasts were a key part of Israel's existence. Passover alone is mentioned more than seventy times. But the problem was that many people know very little about the feasts, which sparked my interest that later developed into a desire to help women understand these annual appointments with God and how they point to His son, Jesus Christ.

This Bible study is for the woman who has never studied Scripture, but it also has insights and information that I believe would be helpful to one who has been studying for some time. It can be done individually or as a group, with women coming together weekly to discuss their individual study. My prayer is that anyone who participates in this study will see just how much God loves us—enough that He planned before creation to send His son to pay the price for sin. And that His love is so great that He continually seeks after a relationship with us.

With the feasts, God invited Israel to meet with Him on appointed days and weeks throughout the year. And with each appointment was revealed a picture of the coming love and work of the Messiah. I hope each one who studies through this workbook will finish with a stronger walk with Jesus Christ.

Romans 15:4 "For whatever was written in former days was written for our instruction, that through endurance and through the encouragement of the Scriptures we might have hope."

Contents

From the Author v

Week 1 - The Lord's Feasts 1
 Day 1 - Introduction 1
 Day 2 - The Passover Feast 6
 Day 3 - Our Passover Lamb 11
 Day 4 - Jesus' final Passover meal 17

Week 2 – Passover Week 25
 Day 1 - Feast of Unleavened Bread 25
 Day 2 - Put Away All Leaven 30
 Day 3 - The Feast of Firstfruits 33
 Day 4 - God First 37

Week 3 - The Feast of Weeks 43
 Day 1 - Shavuot 43
 Day 2 - Lord of the Harvest 46
 Day 3 - Honoring His Word 49
 Day 4 - The Coming of His Spirit 53

Week 4 - Feast of Trumpets 59
 Day 1 - The Day of Blowing Trumpets 59
 Day 2 - The Trumpet signals Alarm 62
 Day 3 - The Shofar 66
 Day 4 - The Last Trumpet 68

Week 5 - The Day of Atonement 71
 Day 1 - The Day 71
 Day 2 - Entering the Holiest Place 73
 Day 3 - The Lord's Goat 78
 Day 4 - The Scapegoat 81

Week 6 - The Feast of Tabernacles 85
 Day 1 - Sukkot 85
 Day 2 - A Joyful Celebration 88
 Day 3 - The Word became Flesh 92
 Day 4 - All Nations will Worship the King 96

Endnotes 101

Week 1 - **The Lord's Feasts**

Day 1 - Introduction

Over the next several weeks we will be looking at the seven feasts dictated by God to Moses in Leviticus 23. The annual feasts were a major part of the Israelites' life in the Old Testament. In just this chapter in Leviticus, the feasts are referred to as "appointed feasts" and "holy convocations," words that indicate these were sacred days intended to express devotion to God. They were appointments on Jehovah's annual calendar when Israel was offered the privilege of meeting with their God. They were also memorial feasts intended to prompt Israel's memory of all the Lord had done for them.

But why should we, who are New Testament Christians, want to study the feasts of the Old Testament at all? Moishe Rosen, founder of Jews for Jesus, explains the "study of the feasts brings one into the bigger picture of how all Scripture—from beginning to end—works together to produce faith in the hearts of those who love God."[1] If we really want to know our God, we need to study both the Old and New Testaments. His character and attributes are seen throughout the Old Testament writings. In Scripture we see the truth, faithfulness and love of God, not to mention His patience. And face it, we like to think we are different than the Jews of old but if we are honest, we are just as foolish and stubborn a people but the difference is we have the capability to learn from someone else's history.

The Old Testament does not just teach us of the character and attributes of God, it also points us to Jesus Christ. After His resurrection, Jesus taught two travelers on the way to Emmaus "beginning with Moses and all the Prophets, He interpreted to them in *all* the Scriptures the things concerning Himself" (Luke 24:27). The apostle Paul wrote "For all the promises of God find their Yes in Him" (2 Cor. 1:20a). It is not just the Old Testament prophecies that point to Christ, but also the writings of Moses, which included the sacrificial system. One of the most important reasons for studying the feasts is that each one points to Christ.

Jesus and his disciples observed the feasts. It was important to Jesus to observe all His Father had commanded of the Jews which included these memorial days. Much of the way scholars have built a time line of Christ's earthly life is by the observances of the feasts.

1

_____

_____

_____

_____

The festivals, or feasts, were "shadows of things to come" meaning they pointed to Christ. They were a picture of the one perfect sacrifice that would bring about the world's hope for redemption and eternity with God. I believe the feasts themselves are proof that God did not decide thousands of years into humanity that He needed a new plan. Christ on the cross was His plan from before creation. As He was bringing Israel out of Egypt and later into the Promised Land, God gave His people the memorial feasts that pointed to our redemption through His Son.

This study is designed with four days of homework each week. I recommend doing the study with a group, coming together once a week to discuss what you may have gleaned from Scripture and the text. The remainder of today's focus is going to be a general introduction and then we will spend the remaining days this week focused on the first of the seven feasts—the Passover.

Please read Leviticus 23.

In this chapter, Moses documents all of the special feasts of the Lord as well as the Sabbath observance. There are a few things we need to take note of concerning the feasts. First, there are seven with the first four feasts of Passover, Unleavened Bread, Firstfruits, and Weeks occurring in the spring of Israel's year. The last three are the feasts of Trumpets, Day of Atonement, and Tabernacles, which are all observed in the fall and all three observed in the seventh month. Second, these were holy appointments the nation of Israel had with God. They were identified as the Lord's feasts, which say they belonged to Him so they were not to be considered as ordinary days, but sacred, holy days. Finally, my prayer is that through this study you will see that each of these feasts not only memorialized something from Israel's history, but also pictured the coming and redemption of Jesus Christ.

Moses actually begins Leviticus 23 with instructions for the Sabbath, which was to be observed weekly, while the seven feasts were to be observed annually. The Sabbath was to be a day of rest when no ordinary work was done. Like the Sabbath, most of the feasts would observe work-free days, thereby making them Sabbath-like.

The first time we see the Sabbath observed is by God at the end of the creation week. Genesis 2:3 states "Then God blessed the seventh day and sanctified it, because in it He rested from all His work which God had created and made" (NASB). God intended for work to occur six days but the seventh was to be a day of rest from any ordinary work. But man later took the Sabbath and made it more of a burden than a rest. The religious men of Israel added many restrictions to the seventh day of the week. However, what they managed to do was put all the emphasis on what people were or were not doing and take it off of God. The observance of the Sabbath was one of the reasons the religious leaders wanted Jesus killed, because He did not follow _their_ Sabbath law.

_____

_____

_____

_____

Jesus told the Pharisees that the Sabbath had been established for man and that _He_ was Lord of the Sabbath. Jesus is Lord of the Sabbath because He is God. In a few verses before, Jesus stated He had the authority on earth to forgive sins. Certainly the one who can forgive sins has authority over the Sabbath. But what does it mean that _the Sabbath was made for man_? It means that God established the Sabbath for our benefit. It was a gift from God to man to help, not hinder or burden him. Rest is important for the physical body to remain healthy, and by doing so, blesses the body. It is also a means of refreshment for our spiritual being. God rested on the first Sabbath possibly as an example to us. Certainly He did not need to rest since the Bible says that God never sleeps (Psalm 121:3, 4), so obviously rest is not a key to His existence, but it is to ours.

In Genesis 2, Moses referenced the day simply as the seventh day. It is not referred to as the Sabbath until Exodus 16.

Exodus 16:23a "[Moses] said to them, 'This is what the Lord commanded: Tomorrow is a day of solemn rest, a holy Sabbath to the Lord . . . '"

Moses was speaking to the leaders of the congregation on the sixth day, explaining that the next day, or the seventh day, was to be a holy day—a Sabbath. The word Sabbath in the Hebrew is 'shabbath' meaning "intermission or the day of rest."[2] In the above passage and Exodus 20:11, it is described as a _holy_ day. Moses wrote ". . . the Lord blessed the Sabbath day and _made it holy_." The Hebrew word for _holy_ is 'qadash' and means "to make or pronounce clean, to dedicate, to consecrate to God, to hallow, to be regarded as holy."[3] In Deuteronomy, Moses states remembering (or keeping/observing) the day _sanctifies_ it and uses the same Hebrew word 'qadash' (Deut 5:12). Douglas Stuart explains "as people keep the Sabbath, stopping their work and devoting themselves to worship, they demonstrate openly that they are keeping the covenant."[4] Keeping the Sabbath, or seventh day of the week, was viewed as a testimony of the covenant between Israel and God.

Please read Exodus 31:12-17 and write all you learn about the Sabbath.

_____

_____

_____

_____

_____

The Sabbath might be considered the most important of the Jewish holy days because it was observed weekly, not just annually, and breaking it was punishable by death. In the explanatory notes of the ESV Study Bible, this passage is explained as reminding Israel "of what the instructions about the tabernacle signify; remembering the Sabbath by keeping it holy is integral to Israel's life as the people who are sanctified (or "made holy") by the Lord."[5]

The Jewish Sabbath was the last day of the week, or Saturday; however, Christians normally worship on Sunday because it is the first of the week and the day of Christ's resurrection. According to the apostle Paul, the day was observed "in honor of the Lord" (Rom 14:6). For the apostle, this was no longer about the law but about personal conviction. But keep in mind that the day was instituted *for man*, and a day of rest is good for the body and soul.

And though we could do an entire study on the Sabbath alone, our concentration for this study is going to be on the seven *annual* feasts ordained in the remainder of Leviticus 23, so we will move on to the first of these feasts. Did you notice when reading Exodus 31 that the Lord commanded Moses to keep His Sabbath*s*, plural? That is because many of the feasts had days that were treated as Sabbaths or days without ordinary work.

The first of the seven feasts mentioned in Leviticus 23 is Passover. The Passover was one of three feasts in which all Jewish males were required to appear before the Lord. In Deuteronomy 16:6, God informs the people that the Passover would no longer be observed in individual homes once they entered the Promised Land but would be observed at a central place of worship of God's choosing.

Exodus 23:14 – 19a (NASB) "Three times a year you shall celebrate a feast to Me. You shall observe the Feast of Unleavened Bread; for seven days you are to eat unleavened bread, as I commanded you, at the appointed time in the month Abib, for in it you came out of Egypt. And none shall appear before Me empty-handed. Also you shall observe the Feast of the Harvest of the first fruits of your labors from what you sow in the field; also the Feast of the Ingathering at the end of the year when you gather in the fruit of your labors from the field. Three times a year all your males shall appear before the Lord GOD. You shall not offer the blood of My sacrifice with leavened bread; nor is the fat of My feast to remain overnight until morning. You shall bring the choice first fruits of your soil into the house of the LORD your God."

What were the three feasts in which all males were to appear before the Lord?

_____

_____

_____

I am sure you noticed the first feast mentioned was not listed as Passover, but the Feast of Unleavened Bread. The Feast of Unleavened Bread actually includes Passover & Firstfruits, while the Feast of Harvest is also called the Feast of Weeks, and the Feast of Ingathering is sometimes referred to as the Feast of Tabernacles or Booths. I know it can get a little confusing. Ultimately, each of these three feasts was celebrated in Jerusalem and all the commanded sacrifices associated with them would occur at the Tabernacle or Temple. I could not find where God explains why they would have to go to a central place for these three feasts, but some think that by requiring the nation to come together physically, they would remain united socially and spiritually. That certainly makes sense because in the wilderness they were all together; however, in the Promised Land, the people would be spread out, so this might have been part of God's plan to keep them united. It certainly is like God to provide beneficial instruction for His people beforehand.

It is important that we understand these feasts were really far more than just simple festivals, they were appointments with God. All seven feasts were days or weeks set apart from all other days to remember and acknowledge the greatness of the Lord and all He had done for His people. They were "divine appointments" on Israel's yearly calendar and three of these appointments would take place in a central worship site, which would later be designated as Jerusalem. The prophet Isaiah actually spoke of Jerusalem as the "city of our appointed feasts" (Is 33:20).

Absolutely key to the Passover feast is the word "remember" (Deut 16:3). The people of Israel were to participate in it as a *memorial* to God's deliverance of their nation from the bondage of slavery. Think for a minute about the very first Passover which took place in Egypt (we will actually look at this in detail tomorrow). The people of Israel were really not a formal nation prior to this time. They were simply the descendants of Abraham, but then God provided these descendants a deliverer in Moses. Along with his older brother Aaron, Moses went before Pharaoh on ten occasions demanding God's people be set free from some 400 years of slavery. But God had made a promise to Abraham more than 400 years before concerning the people's slavery in Egypt.

Genesis 15:13 - 16 (NASB) "God said to Abram, 'Know for certain that your descendants will be strangers in a land that is not theirs, where they will be enslaved and oppressed four hundred years. But I will also judge the nation whom they will serve, and afterward they will come out with many possessions. As for you, you shall go to your fathers in peace; you will be buried at a good old age. Then in the fourth generation they will return here, for the iniquity of the Amorite is not yet complete.'"

How amazing is God! Hundreds of years before Israel is enslaved by Egypt, He tells Abraham about his descendants, the good and the bad. He promised to judge the nation responsible for their bondage and, did you get this, the people would leave their bondage with many possessions.

Read Exodus 12:35-36. What did the Egyptian people do for the Israelite people?

_____

_____

_____

_____

Just as God had promised Abraham, He gave the Israelite people *favor in the eyes of the Egyptians* and they left Egypt with articles of silver, gold and clothing. What other slaves have ever been gifted by their captors then told to please get lost? This is one of those awesome passages (of which there are hundreds) where we see how faithful God is to His Word. What He says He will do we can trust Him to do completely.

The total descendants of Abraham that entered the nation of Egypt in the time of Joseph totaled 70 people (Genesis 46:27), however they left the land hundreds of years later "600,000 soldiers on foot, besides women and children," totaling possibly two million people (Ex 12:37). Here is another promise made to Abraham that God was faithful to keep. Before Abraham had any children, God said to him "Look toward heaven and number the stars, if you are able to number them . . . so shall your offspring be. . ." (Gen 15:5). He promised to make him a great nation and here we see Israel's beginning. They would no longer simply be the descendants of Abraham but the people of God and the nation of Israel. Four generations in Egypt and then the people would be released to the land deeded to Abraham.

God's deliverance is the theme of the Passover Feast. It represents God's love and faithfulness to the people He had chosen, not because they deserved it. No, it was all a matter of God's grace and mercy. On the original Passover day, God passed through Egypt at midnight and took the life of the firstborn of each family and animal where the blood of the sacrificial lamb had not been applied to their home. With this final plague, God released His people from the bondage of Egypt and they exited their bondage to enter into His Promised Land. Just like the Israelites, we have been released from the bondage of sin if we have been saved by the blood of the true Passover Lamb. ". . . For Christ, our Passover lamb, has been sacrificed" (1 Cor 5:7b).

Today has been an introduction into the feasts and a start to our look at Passover. One of my goals with this study is to show that the cross was never a backup plan but the original plan. All that God established with His people in the Old Testament was a means of pointing them to Him and the cross of His Son. My prayer is that if you are not already in love with God's Word, you soon will be simply because His Word is to be treasured.

Deuteronomy 32:46-47 ". . . Take to heart all the words by which I am warning you today, that you may command them to your children, that they may be careful to do all the words of this law. For it is no empty word for you, but your very life, and by this word you shall live long in the land that you are going over the Jordan to possess."

Day 2 - The Passover Feast

Today we are going to look at the original Passover documented for us in Exodus 12. Did you know that the Passover feast is the oldest continuously observed feast in existence today, celebrated for some 3,500 years?[6] The first Passover took place on the night Israel left the bondage of Egypt by God's hand. It was on this original feast day that God sent the final plague of judgment on Egypt. The angel of death came through the land and took the life of the firstborn male in any household that did not have the blood of a lamb on its doorposts.

Every Passover since has been a memorial to remind God's people of His deliverance and the nation of Israel's beginning.

Please read Exodus 12 and answer the following:

What did God change about Israel's religious calendar with Passover?

_____

_____

_____

_____

The instructions for the first Passover begin with the Lord speaking to Moses and his brother Aaron declaring "This month shall be for you the *beginning of months*. It shall be *the first month* of the year *for you*" (Exodus 12:2, emphasis added). Tishri (September/October) would no longer be the first month of the Israel's year; Abib (March/April) would be the first month in their calendar. Notice God says this change is "for you" or for Israel, not Egypt or any other nation. This was a change personal to Israel, setting them apart from Egypt. With this change, Israel would have a religious calendar that would (should) remind them of their nation's beginning. According to Douglas Stuart, "God was teaching them [Israel] to link even their measuring of time to his calling on their lives."[7] Stuart also suggests that God made this change in Israel's calendar to differentiate (or separate) them from the surrounding pagan nations. God did ordain that His people be separate from the other nations.

Leviticus 18:1-4 "And the Lord spoke to Moses saying 'Speak to the people of Israel and say to them, I am the Lord your God. You shall not do as they do in the land of Egypt, where you lived, and you shall not do as they do in the land of Canaan, to which I am bringing you. You shall not walk in their statutes. You shall follow my rules and keep my statutes and walk in them. I am the Lord your God."

Leviticus 20:26 "You [Israel] shall be holy to me, for I the Lord am holy and have separated you from the peoples, that you should be mine."

Israel was a nation of people chosen by God and set apart from all the other nations. I agree with Stuart that the changing of the nation's calendar may have been a means of separating God's people from the other nations. Throughout the books of the Pentateuch (which are the five books attributed to Moses), we can see God working and changing the ways of His people so that they would not be like the other people groups and so that He would be their focus. In order for Israel to be separate or different, God had to be first in their lives. The annual feasts were another means of separating the people from the surrounding nations and keeping their attention on God.

Let's continue by delving further into Exodus 12.

Please complete the following:

On the 10th of this month (Abib/Nisan), every man/household was to take a _____ (Ex 12:3).

The requirements concerning the animal were:

Must be without _____ (Ex 12:5).

A _____ old or in its prime (Ex 12:5).

May be taken from the _____ or goats (Ex 12:5).

They were to keep it until the _____ day of the same month (Ex 12:6).

Not one of its bones were to be _____ (Ex 12:46).

It was to be _____ by fire (Ex 12:8).

They were not to eat it _____ (Ex 12:9).

The lamb was also not to be _____ in water (Ex 12:9).

None of it was to _____ until morning (Ex 12:10).

If any remained, it was to be _____ (Ex 12:10).

The animal was to be killed at _____ (Ex 12:6).

No _____ was to eat of the Passover meal (Ex 12:43, 45).

No _____ male was to eat of the Passover meal (Ex 12:48).

The Passover was to be kept by all of _____ (Ex 12:47).

It was to be a memorial day kept by future _____ (Ex 12:14)

The Passover feast was to be a commemorative meal with the menu and all recipes supplied by the Lord. It was a meal that was to be eaten by the entire household, with one lamb prepared per family. If one lamb were too much for a single family, they were to share the lamb with a neighboring family because this was not to be an individual meal but a family meal.

A lamb was the centerpiece of the meal because if there was no lamb, there would be no deliverance from the final plague. It was the blood of the blemish-free lamb that would protect the first-born of Israel from death. Being a very young animal, only a year-old, symbolized the innocence of this sacrifice. The lamb was to be selected and set aside from the flock on the tenth of the month; however, it was not slaughtered until the fourteenth. Why not just choose the lamb on the day it was to be killed and prepared for the feast? Separating the animal from the rest of flock would allow an opportunity to observe and make sure it was without blemish. The lamb was not to have any flaws; it was to be the best of flock. They were not to offer God their rejects.

Lambs were to be slaughtered at twilight on the 14th day of the month. In the Hebrew the term *twilight* literally means "between the two evenings," a meaning that is sometimes disputed. According to John MacArthur, twilight was determined as the "time between sunset and the onset of darkness or from the decline of the sun until sunset."[8] Most bible scholars believe this to be between 3 pm and 5 pm.[9]

The Lord stated the lamb had to be roasted and eaten along with unleavened bread and bitter herbs. Roasting is thought to be a picture of judgment which fell to the innocent lamb instead of the firstborn male of the household. The meal was to be prepared and eaten in haste (Exodus 12:11) because the people were to be ready to exit Egypt at a moment's notice. They were not sure when they would be leaving; only that they would be leaving and they ate the meal in that manner.

Their quick departure is one reason the bread was to be made without leaven. Leaven is an agent which causes dough to rise, such as yeast, and that required time, time they did not have to wait. They were not just to eat unleavened bread with the Passover meal but for the seven days following, and were also to remove all leaven from their homes on the very first day of the feast week. In verse 17, the Lord gives these seven days a name—the Feast of Unleavened Bread. Even though the Feast of Unleavened Bread is part of Passover, we will be considering the Feast of Unleavened Bread as the second of the seven feasts and will look at it more closely in our second week of study, at which time we will consider leaven.

In reference to the lamb's preparation, God not only said it had to be roasted, He noted that it could not be eaten raw or boiled. Obviously, we understand why it was not to be eaten raw (because that would be totally disgusting and unhealthy), but why not boiled? Well, according to verse 46, none of the lamb's bones were to be broken. Understand I am not certain this is the reason, but boiling meat actually tenderizes even the bones of the animal, which could cause one to weaken enough that it might be broken during preparation. God was providing His people with every opportunity to do exactly as He commanded without any accidental mishaps.

Concerning those who were to participate in the feast, all of Israel was to partake of the meal (12:47). No one was exempt because everyone needed deliverance. Also, God gave very specific instructions concerning any foreigners or slaves—"no uncircumcised person shall eat of it" (12:48). Anyone who participated in the Lord's feast had to be aligned (or identified) with Him, and, in the Old Testament era, that was by circumcision.

***Genesis 17:10-11, 13b** "This is my covenant, which you shall keep, between me and you and your offspring after you: Every male among you shall be circumcised. You shall be circumcised in the flesh of your foreskins, and it shall be a sign of the covenant between me and you. . . So shall my covenant be in your flesh an everlasting covenant."*

Circumcision was the *sign of the covenant* commanded by God of Abraham even before the birth of Isaac. It was another means of setting His people apart from all the pagan nations around them. Circumcision symbolized that the males of Israel and their households were committed to the Lord as the one true God. Those leaving Egypt were not just descendants of Abraham (12:38), so the Lord reminded Moses that they were to be His *covenant* people, and only His covenant people could participate in His feasts. Just as circumcision was an Old Testament requirement, baptism is usually required in many churches in order for someone to participate in the Lord's Supper. Both are signs that a person identifies with Jehovah God and His Son. And with the Lord's feasts, only those who aligned themselves with Him were allowed to participate.

So all of the covenant people of God were to select and prepare a year old, blemish-free lamb and serve it with unleavened bread and bitter herbs (which would remind them of the bitterness of slavery). No uncircumcised male was allowed to eat of the Passover, nor were they to keep any leftovers from the lamb. But there was one other command in connection with the lamb.

> **At the original Passover in Egypt, what was each household to do with the blood of the sacrificed animal?**

_____

_____

_____

_____

Each household was to take some of the blood from the slain animal and put it on the sides and top of their door frames. The lintel was the horizontal beam above the door. This was done in preparation for the tenth and final plague when God would pass through Egypt and take the life of the firstborn of "both man and beast" (Exodus 12:12). This was the plague of judgment against all the gods of Egypt. Each one of the first nine plagues had been against an individual Egyptian god. For example, the Egyptians worshiped a sun god so with the first plague Jehovah God sent darkness over the land. They also worshiped the Nile so He turned the water into blood. But the final plague was an overall judgment aimed at all of the Egyptian gods.

> **Fill in the following, which states what the Israelites were to do to be obedient to God's instructions and what God would then be prompted to do because of their obedience.**

> **Exodus 12:23 "For the Lord will pass through to strike the Egyptians, and when he _____ on the lintel and on the two door posts, the Lord will _____ the door and will not allow the _____ to enter your houses to strike you."**

God told Moses and Aaron that He would see the blood on the doorways, "pass over you," and then they would be saved from death. Hence, the name for the feast is Passover as it was given to memorialize the day of God's deliverance, or the day God *passed over* the firstborn of Israel. But the Egyptians were judged by God just as He had promised.

"At midnight the Lord struck down all the firstborn in the land of Egypt, from the firstborn of Pharaoh who sat on his throne to the firstborn of the captive who was in the dungeon, and all the firstborn of the livestock. And Pharaoh rose up in the night, he and all his servants and all the Egyptians. And there was a great cry in Egypt, for there was not a house where someone was not dead" Exodus 12:29-30.

From the ruler to the prisoner, every firstborn that was not behind the door with the blood of the sacrificial lamb lost his life that night. That is the message of Passover—there is no deliverance without the Passover Lamb. God is a covenant God who is faithful to His Word. Though this feast was instituted for the deliverance of God's people, God gave instructions for its annual observance as a memorial feast when Israel would remember all that God did for His chosen people. That it is by His hand that they are a people, a nation. It is a feast that looks forward to their time in the land promised to them by God. The Passover was just one event that would teach the Jewish people that "the Lord your God is God, the faithful God who keeps covenant and steadfast love with those who love him and keep his commandments, to a thousand generations. . ." (Deuteronomy 7:9). Oh, that we would learn the same truth.

Day 3 - Our Passover Lamb

Today our focus will be on the sacrifice or the lamb. I have to warn you, this is going to be another full day but please do not skip anything.

First I want us to consider why they were to select the lamb on the 10th but not sacrifice it until the 14th. I could not find where God gave any explanation in Scripture but many have speculated. The Israelites were to select and separate the lamb from the flock in order that it might be observed to make certain it was fit for sacrifice, or truly without blemish. But to do this someone in the family, and possibly several members of the family, would have to spend time with the animal and could become attached to it, almost like a pet. It would no longer be considered simply *a* lamb but *their* lamb. Notice the wording used in Exodus 12:3 is "take *a* lamb" but in verse 5 (of the ESV, NASB and King James translations) Moses calls it "*Your* lamb." I believe that it was important that they grasp the fact that there was a cost involved with the sacrifice: an innocent life was taken so that they could be passed over by death. A death occurred in every home in Egypt that night, in the Egyptian homes it was human and in the Israelite homes an animal, but a death all the same.

Some theologians believe the command to select the lamb four days ahead was only for the original Passover because the instruction is only documented in Exodus 12. According to John Sailhamer, Jewish tradition holds that selecting the lamb on the 10th, placing blood on the doorpost and eating the meal in haste were intended only for the original Passover.[10] This is very possible and could be why other passages describing Passover leave these instructions out (i.e., Lev 23:5; Num 28:16; Deut 16:1-8). Whether the selection of the lambs on the tenth of the month occurred once or with every Passover, I believe it still makes the point that this was personal and the shedding of blood was necessary for death to pass over. According to Hebrews 9:22 ". . . under the law almost everything is purified with blood, and without the shedding of blood there is no forgiveness of sins." About a month or so after Israel left Egypt God instructed them that "the life of the flesh is in the blood, and I have given it for you on the altar to make atonement for your souls, for it is the blood that makes atonement by the life" (Lev 17:11). He could have had them mark their doors with anything to identify them as His people but He chose blood, because He said the shedding of blood was the only thing that could identify them for deliverance.

At the end of Day One we closed with Paul's reference to Jesus as *our* Passover (1 Cor 5:7). Today we are going to look at how the Passover lamb was a picture of Christ and His work on the cross. Passover was an annual feast which looked to the redemption of the Messiah.

Read John 1:29 and note the reference to Jesus.

_____

_____

_____

_____

In this passage, John the Baptist refers to the ultimate sacrifice made by Jesus on the cross for our sins. He is the Lamb of God who gave His life to *take away the sin of the world*. The lambs sacrificed on that first Passover night pointed to the one true Lamb of God who met each of the requirements established by God for the perfect sacrifice. Let's do a comparison and see how Jesus fulfilled each of these.

Read the following New Testament passages and note how Jesus fulfilled the Old Testament:

The Passover lambs	Jesus Christ
Ex 12:3 on the 10th to take a lamb	1 Peter 1:20_____
Ex 12:5 without blemish	1 Peter 1:19_____
Ex 12:5 to be a year-old male	Luke 3:23 _____
Ex 12:6 kill the lamb at twilight	Luke 23:44_____
Ex 12:46 were not to break any of its bones	John 19:33 _____

Let's look at each one of these briefly. First, the lambs were to be chosen *before* the Passover date. According to Peter, Jesus was chosen "before the foundation of the world" to be our sacrifice. The apostle John begins his gospel with the fact that Jesus was present and participated in the creation of the world. You could also make a case for His selection by the people. Each of the gospel writers record the account of Jesus' entry into Jerusalem just days before the Passover. The people lined the road waving palm branches and shouting "Hosanna! Blessed is he who comes in the name of the Lord, even the King of Israel!" (John 12:13). Now I realize they had not specifically chosen him to be their *lamb*, however, they were looking to Him for their *deliverance*, and that is exactly what the Lamb of God brought to believers.

The second item was the lamb had to be without blemish or as close to perfect as an earthly lamb could be. They were not to give God their rejects, the lambs they didn't want or the one for which they had no use because the sacrifice was to be worthy of God and I think maybe it was to cost them something. They were to offer to Him only their best. And in the same way, God offered up for us His best. Peter writes that Jesus was offered as a lamb without blemish. The writer of the book of Hebrews states that Jesus "offered himself without blemish to God" (Heb 9:14). He was the only one to ever live a sinless life, so He was the only one who could pay the price for sin. There was no guilt found in Him, he was completely sinless.

And just as the animal was chosen and observed days before it was sacrificed, I want to suggest that Jesus was also observed before His death. He had presented Himself for public ministry at approximately thirty years old and remained in the public eye for more than three years. At no point during this time did anyone find any honest fault with Him. On a couple occasions, the Father even spoke from Heaven of His pleasure in His Son. The writer of Hebrews explains "For we do not have a high priest who is unable to sympathize with our weaknesses, but one who in every respect has been tempted as we are, *yet without sin*" (Hebrews 4:15, emphasis added). The ESV Study Bible footnote explains "though Jesus was tempted in every respect, that is, in every area of personal life, he (unlike every other human) remained sinless . . ."[11]

Think about where He was just days prior to Passover—in Jerusalem. By Jesus' day, each of the lambs to be offered at the Temple had to be examined by the priests to assure it was worthy. Many Jews actually purchased their lambs within the Temple complex to avoid the probability that any lamb brought from outside would be rejected by the priests. I believe that just as the lambs were observed and determined spotless, so was Jesus.

Jesus spent the days prior to Passover in plain view and closely watched by the chief priests and scribes. He taught daily in the Temple where they sent spies to try and catch Him in a lie or reason for arrest, but instead they could only marvel at His teaching (Luke 20:26). Jesus was put through multiple mock trials in an attempt to prove Him guilty of death, yet the only witnesses against Him were liars. Even the priests could find no legitimate fault in Him.

Look at Luke 23:4 and record what Pilate said of Jesus.

_____

_____

_____

Both Pilate and Herod examined Jesus and found Him innocent (Luke 23:14-15). Again, in 1 Peter 1:19 the apostle says Jesus was found to be "without blemish or spot."

Now, the next item requires a little consideration. The lamb had to be male in its first year of life or a young lamb. Of course Jesus was much older than a year but He was young (absolutely young from where I sit). I already noted that He was thirty years old when He began in public ministry and therefore was approximately thirty-three when He died. The lamb chosen for the sacrifice was to be in its prime, as was Christ at His death. I consider thirty-three years to be the prime of life or when someone is hitting their stride. But I also want us to consider the fact that Jesus' ministry began at thirty years old, which I do not believe is a coincidence or random occurrence.

Read the following Old Testament passages and record the position and age specified:

Numbers 4:3, 30 _____

Genesis 41:46 _____

2 Samuel 5:4 _____

Ezekiel 1:1 _____

Of course, only the office of priest had specific age instructions commanded for all Levites who entered that position. I can find nowhere in Scripture that specifically says a king or prophet of God had to be thirty years old. Though the other passages you referenced were not commands concerning the age of rulers or prophets, I find it interesting that some of the men who held these offices and served them well were all thirty when they entered the position.

But why does this matter?

Hebrews 3:1; 5:5-6 _____

Revelation 19:16 _____

Acts 3:19-26 (Deut. 18:15) _____

Jesus holds all three of these offices: prophet, priest and king. The fact that He started His ministry at thirty follows exactly with God's Word. There was not anything about Jesus Christ's life that was random, but everything had to do with the fulfillment of God's plan and glory. I believe the Old Testament points us to Jesus as the one true Messiah and the fulfillment of each of God's stipulations is proof of who He is and why He came to earth.

But we cannot stop here because there is still more in our comparison of Jesus with the Passover lamb. The lamb was to be killed at twilight. We saw on Day Two that twilight was probably between the hours of 3 and 5 pm and was when the lambs were killed. Three of the gospels state that while Jesus was on the cross between the sixth and ninth hour it became dark and at the ninth hour Christ gave up His life. The Jewish day began at 6 am, which would be considered the first hour of the day. Therefore, the ninth hour of the day would be 3 pm, which means that Jesus was on the cross and died at the time the lambs were slaughtered for Passover. That is exactly what we should expect, that the true Passover Lamb would die at the appointed time.

I want to look further at the darkness that fell between the sixth and the ninth hour just before Jesus gave up His life. Matthew, Mark and Luke all point out that "there was darkness over the whole land for three hours" and then Jesus died on the cross (Matthew 27:45, Mark 15:33, Luke 23:44). In Scripture, darkness often represents the judgment of God. Darkness was one of the ten plagues that God brought upon the nation of Egypt in order to persuade Pharaoh to release the people from bondage. I think it is very interesting that darkness was the ninth plague and the one just before the judgment on all the firstborn males (the original Passover).

Exodus 10:22 ". . . there was pitch darkness in all the land of Egypt three days. . ."

Just prior to the institution of Passover, the slaughtering of the lambs and the redemption of Israel, God brought darkness on all the land of Egypt for three days. Thousands of years later, He brought darkness on all the land of Israel for three hours before the True Passover Lamb's death. With the first Passover, darkness preceded as judgment on Egypt. But with the Passover of God's true Lamb, darkness preceded His death as a witness of the horror that fell on this sacrifice, which was all the sins of all time placed upon Him and God's judgment for those sins. In both instances, we see God's wrath poured out on sin.

Read the following verse and write out what Paul calls Jesus.

1 Timothy 2:6 "[He] gave himself as a ransom for all, which is the testimony given at the proper time."

_____

_____

_____

In Galatians 1:4, what does Paul say Jesus delivered us from?

_____

_____

_____

Galatians 1:4 "[He] gave himself for our sins to deliver us from the present evil age, according to the will of our God and Father."

Paul writes that in the same way the Passover lambs ransomed the life of the firstborn males in Egypt, by His death Jesus ransomed us from the judgment of God that, like the Egyptians, we deserved. And in the same way that God delivered Israel from the evil of bondage forced on them by Egypt, Christ gave Himself to 'deliver us from the present evil age.' I have often had people tell me that they do not believe the Bible is anything more than man's imagination. Well, I appreciate that some men have great talent but no group of men over thousands of years could get this right.

But we are still not quite done with our comparisons. The last comparison we need to look at concerns the Passover lamb not having any bones broken. When Christ was on the cross, the Pharisees wanted the legs of all three men broken in order to speed up their deaths so they could be taken down before the actual time the Sabbath would begin (or 6 pm). Breaking the legs of someone on a cross would mean they could not push themselves up in order to breathe, basically causing them to suffocate. This is just one more reason that crucifixion was considered such a horrible, painful death.

The key point here is that the Roman soldiers in charge, who were experts at crucifixion, determined that Jesus was already dead and so they did not break His legs but they did break the legs of the other two men on either side of Jesus.

John 19:32-33 "So the soldiers came and broke the legs of the first, and of the other who had been crucified with him. But when they came to Jesus and saw that he was already dead, they did not break his legs."

Now there are many skeptics who believe that many of the prophecies Jesus fulfilled He staged, but someone explain to me how He could have staged them not breaking His legs before removing Him from the cross. If they did not believe He was God but believed He deserved to die on a cross, they certainly were not going to be taking requests from Him before they murdered Him.

> **Read John 19:36 and record what John said was the reason Jesus' legs were not broken.**

_____

_____

_____

He fulfilled every point of the Old Testament that was written about His first coming, and the unbroken bones were one of those fulfillments.

At the original Passover, it was the blood of many lambs placed on each door frame that provided the people's protection from God's judgment of death. It was the blood of the lamb that brought salvation to the Israelite people. Without it there could be no pass over, no deliverance, only death. And without the true Lamb of God our lives would have no hope for eternity.

Before we end this day I want to share with you something Cecil and Moishe Rosen point out in their book <u>Christ in the Passover</u>. They explain that a ditch was dug in front of the doorway of Egyptian homes to avoid flooding. "The Israelites killed their Passover lambs right by the doors and the blood from the slaughter automatically ran into the depression of the basin at the threshold. When they spread the blood with the hyssop brush, they first touched the lintel (the top horizontal part of the door frame), then each side post (the vertical sides). In doing this, they went through the motions of making the sign of a bloody cross, the prophecy of another Passover sacrifice to come centuries later. Thus, the door was 'sealed' on all four sides with the blood of the lamb, because the blood was already in the basin at the bottom."[12] I have read different commentators relate the door post with blood appearing as a cross but never understood how marking the lintel and posts did that. The Rosen's view is to think of where Jesus' blood would be on the cross. At the top where the crown of thorns went into His head, at the sides where the nails were driven in His hands and at the bottom where the nails were placed in his feet, as well as where the blood would drop from His pierced side. So it is not a cross so much as the blood pattern of someone on a cross. That makes so much more sense to me.

The Passover in Egypt was a complete picture of our salvation. I also believe it is proof that God's plan for salvation was not an afterthought but planned out before the creation of this world. That makes His love so much greater, because it says that even though He knew we would not keep His Law, He set out a plan for our redemption. He loved us even though He knew we would never be worthy of it on our own. That is unconditional love. That is amazing beyond words.

Day 4 - Jesus' final Passover meal

Well, we have made it through three days and hopefully you are not frustrated with me. I do hope you have observed something in the past three days you were not aware of, something that caused you to pause or give you awe over the amazing God we serve. Just the fact that the Father, Son and Holy Spirit decided, before they ever created this world, to provide me a hope and way to heaven is overwhelming for me. Christ loved us, desired relationship with us and was willing to temporarily give up heaven, come to earth, and give up His own life in order to secure our eternity. That is love beyond my finite mind.

In His final hours on earth, Jesus observed the Passover feast with His disciples. He told them that He had earnestly desired to eat that Passover meal with them (Luke 22:15). Let's take a look at this passage in the New Testament which records Jesus' final Passover meal.

Please read Luke 22:14-22.

Here "the hour had come" to celebrate the feast but also for the suffering and death of the Messiah. A number of times the gospel writers note that Jesus' hour had not yet come, such as at the Wedding in Cana (John 2:4) or when the religious leaders tried to arrest Him in the temple (John 7:30; 8:20). But at this final Passover meal, the hour had finally arrived for Jesus "to depart out of this world to the Father . . ." (John 13:1). In the above passage in Luke's gospel, Jesus was about to participate in Passover in a way no one else could, He was going to become *the* sacrificial lamb. Passover was a memorial feast, one which caused the Israelite people to remember how God redeemed their nation out of bondage so that they could be His people and serve Him. It was during this last Passover meal that Jesus instituted a new memorial, the Lord's Supper.

Jesus told the disciples they were to do it *in remembrance* of Him and His death on the cross. He used the unleavened bread of the meal to represent His body, which was the fulfillment of the Passover lamb. The cup, believed to have been the third of the four cups served at Passover, represents His blood that would be shed for our deliverance just hours after this meal. Some religions teach that when we take communion we are literally partaking of His body. But Jesus was speaking figuratively and not saying it was literally His body. The Aramaic actually gives more the sense of *this bread represents me*. He gave thanks for the bread, broke it and then distributed it among His disciples. The broken bread is "called the 'Afikoman' which is from the Greek participle *aphikomenos*, meaning 'the one who comes' . . . Jesus has identified himself as the 'Afikoman,' that is, as 'he who comes,' the Messiah. In accepting and eating the Afikoman, thus identified, the disciples demonstrate their faith in Jesus as the Messiah."[13]

In John 6, it was just before Passover and after Jesus had fed the five thousand when a crowd of people came looking for Him and for a sign (amazing since He just fed five thousand with a couple fish and a few rolls, what more of a sign could we want?). They pointed out how Moses had given their ancestors bread from heaven when in the wilderness. Jesus corrected them by saying ". . . it was not Moses who gave you the bread from heaven, but my Father gives you the *true bread* from heaven. For the bread of God is he who comes down from heaven and gives life to the world . . . I am the bread of life; whoever comes to me shall not hunger, and whoever believes in me shall never thirst. . . For this is the will of my Father, that everyone who looks on the Son and believes in him should have eternal life, and I will raise him up on the last day. . . I am the *living bread* that came down from heaven. If anyone eats of this bread, he will live forever. And the bread that I will give for the life of the world is my flesh. . . Truly, truly, I say to you, unless you eat the flesh of the Son of Man and drink his blood, you have no life in you. Whoever feeds on my flesh and drinks my blood has eternal life, and I will raise him up on the last day. For my flesh is true food, and my blood is true drink. Whoever feeds on my flesh and drinks my blood abides in me, and I in him" (John 6:32-33, 35, 40, 51, 53-56, emphasis added).

Before the institution of the Lord's Supper, Jesus explained that His flesh and blood would be offered up as a sacrifice for all but only those who would partake would have eternal life. At the time of this teaching all who heard it had difficulty understanding because they took Him literally. Even many of His disciples stated "This is a hard saying; who can listen to it?" and many left Him (6:60, 66). But the Twelve chose to remain because, as Peter stated, Jesus had *the words of eternal life* (6:68). And, at their final Passover together, they received the bread and wine symbolically of their faith in Christ.

_____

_____

_____

_____

Paul wrote that by participating in the Lord's Supper we *proclaim His death until he comes.* When we take of the Lord's Supper we remember what He did on the cross for our sins and that He will return in glory as King. Jesus died on the cross for our sins, rose from the dead on the third day, ascended to heaven in a cloud and will return for His church to reign forever. Hallelujah, we serve a risen Savior!

I cannot leave this passage in 1 Corinthians without noting the phrase "as often as you eat this bread and drink the cup" because we don't always eat of it often. Even though Jesus did not command any specifics as to how often we participate in this ordinance, the wording Paul uses seems to indicate more often than less. Just the fact that we are to do this in remembrance of Christ and the importance of what He did for us would intimate that we observe the Lord's Supper often. I have to admit that there was a time when I thought that since the various feasts were only once a year, maybe the Lord's Supper should be observed annually (at the time my church observed it on the first Sunday of every month). But now I believe that as often as we desire to observe it, we should, whether it is monthly, weekly, whenever. We must be careful to realize the seriousness of this ordinance.

1 Corinthians 11:27-29 "Whoever, therefore, eats the bread or drinks the cup of the Lord in an unworthy manner will be guilty concerning the body and blood of the Lord. Let a person examine himself, then, and so eat of the bread and drink of the cup. For anyone who eats and drinks without discerning the body eats and drinks judgment on himself."

According to commentator John Phillips, "the word translated 'unworthy' is *anaxios*, occurring only here (verse 27) and verse 29. It means to participate in the Lord's Supper without proper preparation. The warning may have reference to the unsaved; although it is difficult to see how a person can remember one he does not even know. The warning certainly has reference to believers. We are not to participate at the Lord's Table lightly or flippantly. . . Paul underlines how serious a matter it is to partake of the emblems at the Lord's Supper in an unworthy way. Such a person becomes guilty of the body and blood of the Lord."[14] To emphasize the seriousness, Paul actually repeats the warning again later in the same chapter. It is no wonder that many churches guard this ordinance; as well they should, by requiring those participating to be baptized believers, some even requiring that they be members of their congregation. I tend to agree with my local congregation, that anyone who professes to be a believer may participate and I base this on Paul's statement that we are to each *examine ourselves* (11:28a). It is the *Lord's* table and He will see to the truths of it. But we need to examine our own hearts before we partake, confess any sin, and focus on Him when we come to His table, remembering who He is and what He has done for us.

I believe that parents should begin early in their children's lives teaching them the importance of this ordinance. During the Passover meal, the youngest child asks a series of questions concerning the origination of the ordinance and their ancestors' deliverance from Egypt. This tradition probably stems from the Lord's instruction that "when your children say to you, 'What do you mean by this service?' you shall say, 'It is the sacrifice of the Lord's Passover, for he passed over the houses of the people of Israel in Egypt, when he struck the Egyptians but spared our houses'" (Exodus 12:26-27). The origination and symbolism of the Lord's Supper can be taught the same way.

But the Lord's Supper was not the only thing Jesus instituted with this feast.

What does Jeremiah 31: 31, 34 promise?

_____

_____

_____

_____

With the third cup of the Passover, which was the cup of blessing, Jesus announced the beginning of the New Covenant—"This cup that is poured out for you is the new covenant in my blood" (Luke 22:20). The bread and the cup represented "the once-for-all-fulfillment of the ceremonies surrounding the Passover lamb."[15] Jesus' blood was the sacrificial blood that would seal the New Covenant just as blood of a sacrifice was used by Moses to seal the Old Testament covenant at Sinai.

Exodus 24:8 "And Moses took the blood and threw it on the people and said, 'Behold the blood of the covenant that the LORD has made with you in accordance with all these words.'"

As far back as Abraham's day, a covenant could not be completed without a death because blood was required to seal it, almost like a signature today. When the people pledged their obedience to the Lord's covenant, Moses sealed or consecrated the covenant by sprinkling half the blood from the sacrifice on the altar and half on the people. We are not given specific information as to why He did this but it may have been a visual for the people of their cleansing and uniting with God.

If we glance back further in the Old Testament, we see the covenant God made with Abraham.

Please read Genesis 15:8-21.

Abraham (or Abram as he was known prior to God changing his name) was told to bring five animals to the Lord: a heifer, a goat, a ram, a turtledove and a pigeon. He cut each of the first three animals (not the birds) in half and laid the pieces opposite each other, making a pathway of blood. A deep sleep came over Abram and God spoke to him of his descendants' future. Then "a smoking firepot and a flaming torch passed between the pieces" (Gen 15:17b). With the passing through the pieces and blood of the sacrifices, God made a covenant with Abraham promising the land of Israel to his descendants. But they would not receive the land until after they had been enslaved in Egypt. This covenant with Abraham was an unconditional covenant and foreshadowed the covenant made with Moses at Sinai. Notice how the Lord's opening statements for the two are almost identical.

Complete and compare the following verses:

Genesis 15:7 "And he said to him, 'I am the _____ who _____ you _____ from _____ of the _____ to give you this _____ to _____.'"

Exodus 20:2 "I am the _____ your God, who _____ you _____ of the land _____, out of the house of slavery."

When the Lord came down on Mount Sinai so the people could hear Him speak and would believe Moses concerning the covenant, the mountain was "wrapped in smoke because the Lord had descended on it in fire. The smoke of it went up like the smoke of a kiln, and the whole mountain trembled greatly" (Exodus 19:18). See any similarity to the covenant account with Abraham? The Lord appeared to Abraham as a *smoking fire pot* and a *flaming torch* passing through the blood. According to John Sailhamer, "It is part of the overall strategy of the book to show that what God did at Sinai was part of a larger plan which had already been put into action with the patriarchs. Thus, the exodus and the Sinai covenant serve as reminders not only of God's power and grace but also of God's faithfulness. What he sets out to accomplish with his people, he will carry through to the end."[16]

The Old Covenant given to Moses and the people of Israel was different than the covenant God made with Abraham. With this covenant He put a condition on the people.

Exodus 19:5-6a "Now therefore, if you will indeed obey my voice and keep my covenant, you shall be my treasured possession among all peoples, for all the earth is mine; and you shall be to me a kingdom of priests and a holy nation."

If the people were obedient and did not follow false gods, the Lord would keep this covenant. This was established as a fulfillment of the covenant made with Abraham and to set Israel apart from all the other nations as a people holy and special to God. Moses was the mediator of the covenant which was between God and His chosen people. Though the people agreed to do *all the Lord had spoken* (Ex 19:8), they were not obedient and did follow false gods, yet this was no surprise to God. Because of this

He had planned for a New Covenant to be instituted by the blood of His Son before the world's creation.

Something I found interesting is that after Moses threw the blood on the people (Ex 24:8), he and the elders ascended the mountain at the Lord's invitation to participate in a covenant meal with Him. In the same respect, the Lord's Supper is a time when the church unites together in the New Covenant with Him.

> **Read Hebrews 9:15-21 and note anything you see on covenant or blood?**

_____

_____

_____

_____

Jesus is the mediator of this New Covenant that is eternal and is instituted based on the shedding of His blood. Another word that could be used in place of covenant is testament. When we think of testament, we usually think of Last Will and Testament, which could be applied here. One thing we see in this passage is there cannot be an inheritance without a death because a will is only enforced when the maker of the will dies. With Jesus' last will and testament He leaves to all those who believe in Him eternal life, a covenant guaranteed by His shed blood on the cross. His blood was shed so that we might be saved from our sins under the first covenant, a covenant of law that we, in and of ourselves, could not keep but can be redeemed from because He paid the price required for our sins.

Three things occurred with the Old Covenant: the law was read, the people agreed, and then it was ratified by the blood and the covenant was in place. Many do not like to hear about blood in the Bible, particularly of Christ's blood. But here is the problem—blood is necessary to deal with the horrible reality of sin. In the Old Testament, thousands of years before Christ, Moses was teaching the Israelites that death was the only way to life. The Lord had the people choose one lamb days before it was to be sacrificed so it would become their personal lamb because salvation is personal. It requires that we engage in a covenant relationship with our God and accept the blood of His Son as our cleansing, which means we have to accept that we need cleansing. We need a personal Savior whose Spirit resides within us and seals us in eternal covenant with our Lord.

Just as the Passover was given to Israel as a memorial or means of remembering all that Jehovah God had done to deliver them and make them His people, the Lord's Supper is given to the church so that we will continually remember what Christ has done for us. The Lord desires relationship with His people and that we would know just how much He loves us. He loves us enough to take the place of the Passover lamb, and died so that we might live. I am continually amazed at the lengths God went to in order to keep His people on track. And how so many hundreds and hundreds of years earlier, He gave us a picture of His plan, the plan that sent His Son to dwell among us and bring to us the gift of eternity. Because of this gift, those who believe in Jesus Christ as Lord and Savior are passed over by eternal death, and given eternal life. Amazing!

I want to leave you this week with a prayer straight from Scripture:

"Now may the God of peace who brought again from the dead our Lord Jesus, the great shepherd of the sheep, by the blood of the eternal covenant, equip you with everything good that you may do his will, working in us that which is pleasing in his sight, through Jesus Christ, to whom be glory forever and ever. Amen" (Hebrews 13:20-21).

Week 2 – **Passover Week**

Day 1 - Feast of Unleavened Bread

Last week we studied the Passover and with it God commanded three items be a part of their meal—the lamb, bitter herbs and unleavened bread. We put our focus on the lamb last week because it is central to Passover. Unleavened bread was a commanded item for both the Passover meal and the Feast of Unleavened Bread, so we will look at it in detail with this week's study.

Because the Feast of Unleavened Bread and Passover occurred consecutively they actually came to be one festival, along with the Feast of Firstfruits, which occurs within the same week. Often in Scripture, these feasts are not listed separately but together, so when one is listed all are usually implied.

> **Please read Leviticus 23:5-6 and write out the dates for**
> **Passover and the Feast of Unleavened Bread.**

_____

_____

_____

> **Now read Exodus 12:16-18 and note how the dates are given.**

_____

_____

Notice in Leviticus, the two feasts are given distinct dates, referencing them as two separate feasts. However, in Exodus there does not seem to be any distinction between the two feasts, it actually seems that they are one event. When you read about Passover in the New Testament, the text usually is referencing the entire week and including all three feasts. The same is true of the Feast of Unleavened Bread, when it is mentioned Passover is usually included.

Matthew 26:17 "Now on the first day of Unleavened Bread the disciples came to Jesus, saying, 'Where will you have us prepare for you to eat the Passover?'"

In this passage, Matthew speaks of eating the Passover on the first day of the Feast of Unleavened Bread because these feasts were considered one. The three feasts, Passover, Unleavened Bread, and Firstfruits, occurred on consecutive days, the 14th, 15th and 16th of the first month (Abib/Nisan), so it was very natural to consider them as one festival. Yet there were specific instructions for each one.

In the passages in Exodus and Leviticus documenting the instructions for the Feast of Unleavened Bread, Moses tells the people that all bread was to be unleavened (which is where the name of the feast originates) from the fourteenth of the first month until the twenty-first day of that month.

> **According to Leviticus 23:6-8, what was different about the first and last days of the week of Unleavened Bread?**

_____

_____

_____

_____

The seven annual feasts were holy appointments with God. The Feast of Unleavened Bread was to begin *and* end with a holy convocation or holy assembling of the people. The word translated *convocation*, or assembly in some translations, is *miqra'* in Hebrew and literally means 'a calling together.'[17] These days of assembling were to be special days of worship when the people were not distracted by routine things but focused on the specialness of God. Several years ago when my son Sean began attending Liberty University, he would talk about attending Convo during the week. Liberty University requires their students to come together for a Holy Convocation (or assembly) three mornings a week to worship and focus on God as a community. It is one of the key things I really like about this college—that my children (my youngest daughter attends now) have been given the opportunity to hear some amazing Bible teachers and Christian authors. It also shows these college students that we can come together for worship more than just weekends. Like the Israelites, when we come together for our worship service, we should consider it a *holy* assembling before the Most Holy God and focus on Him, not ourselves.

The first and last days of the week of this second feast were to be observed differently from the other days.

According to Leviticus 23:8, what were the people to do every day of that week?

_____

_____

_____

The first and last days of this feast were actually to be observed in a *Sabbath-way* having no ordinary work. And for the full week, they were to present a food offering to the Lord *by fire* (Lev 23:8). These were offerings made in addition to their daily offerings. We need to look at the specific offerings commanded for this feast week, so we will look at a passage in the book of Numbers. Numbers is the fourth of the five books written by Moses. These five books are collectively called the Pentateuch, labeled by the Jews as the Torah (which in Hebrew means teaching or instruction, in English Bibles the books are commonly called 'Law').[18] The word Pentateuch is taken from two Greek words, *penta* and *teuchos*. The first means 'five' and teuchos means 'vessel or container.'[19] In other words, these five books are five vessels holding God's revelation (Word) to His people. I love this because I believe this is how we are to consider all of Scripture, as God's Word revealed to His people.

Seriously, I believe this is huge to Christianity and sets it apart from all other religions. Every time you see in Scripture that the Lord spoke to someone or that God said anything, pause to consider the fact that we do not have to speculate about who our God is or what He desires. He has told us all we need to know, we do not have to guess or assume anything. It has been revealed in Scripture from His spoken word.

I want to move into the book of Numbers, in which Moses documents the Israelites' forty years of wilderness wandering before entering the Promised Land. In this book, we are given further instructions for observing the feasts, when the people remember God's mercy to them.

Look at Numbers 28:18-24 and record what the people were to offer on the first day of the feast.

_____ bulls   _____ rams (v19)

_____ male lambs   who would be without _____ (v19)

A _____ offering of fine flour mixed with _____ (v20)

For a bull _____ ephah   a ram _____ ephah (v20)

For each of the lambs _____ ephah (v21)_____ male goat

for a _____ offering to make _____ for you (v22)

The commands for these offerings were given before the people entered the Promised Land and after the office of the priest had been established. These offerings were not part of the earlier written explanation recorded for the Feast of Unleavened Bread, although may have been verbalized by Moses to the people at that time.

On the first day of this feast, the people were to offer eleven animals: two bulls, one ram, seven male lambs, and one male goat. The goat was a sin offering, while the other animals were burnt offerings. Along with the animals, grain offerings specific for each animal were brought consisting of fine flour mixed with oil. And the offerings were to be in addition to, not as a substitute for, the regular daily offerings which were a lamb along with a grain and drink offering in the morning and the same at twilight. Though the first day of the week was to be a holy day without regular work, the priests would be busy with the sacrifices. However, they are not ordinary sacrifices and this should not be considered *regular* work or even work at all. It was an offering made to the Lord and part of their worship. These sacrifices actually set the day apart from other days.

Let's look further at what God commanded concerning this second feast.

Read Exodus 12:15-18; 13:3-7 and fill in the following:

The Israelites were to eat unleavened bread _____ days (12:15).

On the first day, they were to _____ leaven from their _____ (12:15).

Anyone who ate leaven was to be _____ from Israel (12:15, 19).

The feast was to be observed as an _____ (12:17).

Unleavened bread was to be eaten from the _____ until the _____ of Abib (12:18).

On the seventh day, there was to be a _____ to the _____ (13:6).

They were not to have leaven in all their _____ (13:7).

For seven days the Israelites were not to eat *any* bread with leaven. But why couldn't their bread have leaven? I believe there are a couple reasons for this. First, leaven is a substance, like yeast, used to ferment dough causing it to rise. Bread *with* leaven was actually preferred because it tasted better and was more filling. Without leaven, the bread was basically a cracker sheet, dry and crusty. The problem on the day they left Egypt was the Jews did not have time to wait for their dough to rise because they needed to be ready to leave at a moment's notice. And during the following days of that week, they would be traveling to the Promised Land, still moving quickly to avoid their enemy.

_____

_____

_____

It was a meal to be eaten *in haste* because they did not know when the Lord would instruct them to leave, but when they did leave, it would have to be quickly. There would be no time to allow their dough to rise, so the bread would have to be made without leaven. The same would be true for the entire first week or so, as they fled Egypt. There would be no time to wait on bread dough.

Actually bread made without leaven was not just served with the feasts. In Genesis 19, Moses notes that Lot served the Lord's angels unleavened bread probably because he did not know they were coming and prepared the meal quickly. In the New King James, the third verse in that passage actually states Lot "made them a *feast*, and baked unleavened bread and they ate." Even in haste, Lot prepared a proper meal for his guests (also cf. Judges 6:19, 1 Samuel 28:24).

Still, even though unleavened bread was served on unique occasions, the people's preference and custom was to serve bread with leaven for their meals. It does not seem likely that they would voluntarily eat it for seven straight days. The unleavened bread that the people would eat for a full week every year would remind them of their hasty departure from Egypt. Moses told the people that they would tell their children "'It is *because* of what the LORD did for me when I came out of Egypt.'... For with a strong hand the Lord has brought you out of Egypt. You shall therefore keep this statute at its appointed time from *year to year*" (Exodus 13:8b, 9b, 10; emphasis added).

We see with the word *ordinance* that this was not optional. Other translations use the word *statute*. But no matter the translation the meaning is clear, this was to be an *annual* celebration *commanded* by God. They were to remember every year of how God had saved them from their bondage. With the Exodus, the people were leaving behind a life of bondage under a foreign ruler and headed to a life of freedom under the rule of a holy God—their God. This feast was to remind the generations to come of the original quick departure and miraculous deliverance by God's hand. Eating unleavened bread for seven days was intended to drive the idea into their hearts and minds.

Just as with the Passover feast, the Feast of Unleavened Bread was given to the people of Israel as a means of remembering the greatness of their God and the birth of their nation. This feast is really an act of grace on God's part to His people, truly a gift. He so loves His people and desires only good for them that He established annual feasts to draw their minds and hearts back to Him. He is so faithful and merciful!

We have looked briefly at why they were to eat unleavened bread. Tomorrow, we will continue to look at this because I think from the passage in Exodus 12, we can see that a hasty departure is not the only reason for unleavened bread, but we will leave that for tomorrow.

Day 2 - Put Away All Leaven

Yesterday, we began our study of the Feast of Unleavened Bread and I think we got a good start. Today we are going to continue looking at why the bread had to be leaven-free. We know they had to leave Egypt in haste and did not have time for the dough to rise. Yet, that does not seem to be the only reason because not only were they to eat *un*leavened bread, they also were instructed to *remove all leaven* from their homes on the first day until the seventh day *and* to remove it from their territory or borders. I want to submit to you that the absence of leaven served another purpose.

In Scripture, leaven is often a symbol of sin, corrupt doctrine or evil influence. Throughout their history God intended for the Jews to be a people separate, or different, from the pagan nations surrounding them. The Lord told them "Consecrate yourselves, therefore, and be holy, for I am the LORD your God. Keep my statutes and do them. I am the LORD who sanctifies you" (Lev 20:7-8). Removing all leaven during the feast week was a picture of removing sin from the people's lives.

So the term leaven was sometimes a metaphor for sin. To see this, let's look at a couple New Testament passages that address leaven.

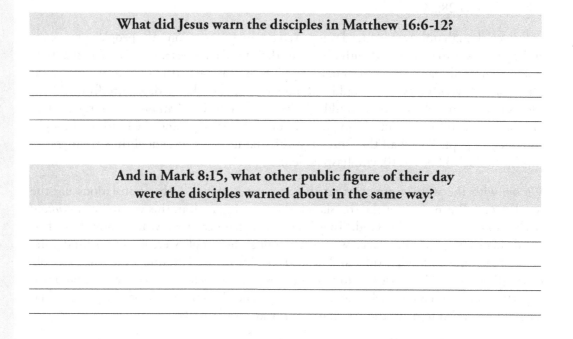

What did Jesus warn the disciples in Matthew 16:6-12?

_____

_____

_____

_____

And in Mark 8:15, what other public figure of their day were the disciples warned about in the same way?

_____

_____

_____

_____

The disciples were confused at first thinking Jesus was speaking of actual bread because He used the word *leaven*. But they soon realized, with a little help, that he was really warning them of the hypocrisy or false teachings of the religious leaders of their day. In Mark 8, He also warned them of the *leaven of Herod*. The religious leaders presented false teaching to the people and displayed hypocritical lives (their leaven). Herod, on the other hand, lived an immoral, corrupt public life, certainly not one that should be imitated.

The Hebrew word for *leavened* is 'chometz' and it means "to be sour, to be embittered, grieved, to be cruel, oppress, to be ruthless"[20] (Ex 12:19). Leaven is a substance, like yeast, that produces fermentation in dough. It causes dough to rise or expand in volume. In that era, there were different ways dough was leavened. One was by dipping it in wine or vinegar, then airing it in the sun. It would then be covered and stored until it soured. Another way was to knead the flour and water with salt until it was a porridge-like consistency, then cover it until it soured. When making bread, a small piece of leavened raw dough saved from a previous batch, or *starter dough,* would be added into new ingredients.[21] With this method, each loaf of bread was really connected to previous batches. But any bread made without the fermented dough would be separated from previous batches. Do you get the picture?

God had commanded the Israelites to remove all leaven from their homes and territory. He was serious about His people being set apart from the world. This required that they symbolically and literally leave Egypt behind them *in Egypt,* and not take it with them. When they left their bondage, they were to leave their old life behind and leaving the leaven was a symbol of this. They were to no longer be connected to the *old chunk of dough.* But it wasn't just the presence of the leaven that was a concern.

What did God say about anyone who ate leaven during the seven days (Ex. 12:15)?

_____

_____

_____

_____

_____

Just as leaven spreads through the dough and increases in volume, sin can spread among people. It is real easy to take on someone else's bad attitude or to jump on the gossip train. We can so easily get sucked into sin or pull other people into our sin. In the same way the Israelites were to leave the old ways in Egypt, believers are to put away old ways, or sins, and live sanctified lives in Christ through His Spirit. We are to step away from anything that will draw us into what we know is not Christ-like.

Read 1 Corinthians 5:6-8 and note what Paul wrote concerning leaven.

_____

_____

_____

According to John MacArthur, Paul is explaining that "when tolerated, sin will permeate and corrupt the whole" church.[22] Solomon wrote that "one sinner destroys much good" (Eccl 9:18). Today New Testament Christians do not celebrate the Feast of Unleavened Bread as the Jews, however, we do (should) celebrate Christ by living *unleavened* lives. Just as God wanted the Israelites to live different lives from what they had seen from the

Egyptians and surrounding people groups, the New Testament church is a *new batch* created without leaven and we are to live like it-different from the world around us. But how are we able to live different lives within the world?

According to Paul what *are* we in Christ (2 Cor. 5:17)?

_____

_____

_____

In Christ, we are redeemed into new creations and are to leave our old lives and ways behind. Living lives that are holy and different from the world is a teaching that runs throughout the Bible for God's people (Old and New Testament). Even with this feast, Israel was not to include any foreigners, all their servants were to be circumcised, and all of Israel was required to participate (Ex 12:44). This was an appointment with Jehovah God for those who were truly His people, separate from those who did not follow Him. Yet God did allow for the stranger who wished to participate but with one stipulation.

What was that stipulation (Exodus 12:48)?

_____

_____

_____

Before any male could participate in the feast, they had to first be circumcised. He demanded that "no uncircumcised person shall eat" the feast. We saw in week one of this study that circumcision was the sign of the covenant given to Abraham in Genesis 17 and it distinguished those who believed in the promises of Holy God from those who did not. It was to designate the Israelites as descendants of Abraham and the people of God, separate and set apart from all other people. Only those set apart for God who believed in His promises were to participate in the feasts. These were to be observed as *everlasting ordinances,* or to be observed forever, by the *true* people of God, and circumcision was the outward sign or proof.

This became a huge issue for New Testament believers with many Jews believing all Gentiles who received Christ as Savior must be circumcised. But Paul wrote that "circumcision is a matter of the heart, by the Spirit, not by the letter" (Romans 2:29b). And he also stated "neither circumcision counts for anything, nor uncircumcision, but a new creation" (Galatians 6:15). It is a heart matter. Paul taught that circumcision was the sign of the Old Covenant. But Christians are under the New Covenant, sealed by the blood of Christ. We have received the Spirit of God who resides in our hearts and enables us to learn and live out Christ's lives. King David asked God to create a new heart within him because David understood that was central to his relationship with God (Psalm 51:10).

For the week of this feast, the Israelites were to purge their homes of all leaven. To me, this is a picture of how we are to allow the Spirit to purge our hearts, creating a new heart within us because we are the home or temple of Christ. Charles Spurgeon said the purifying of the homes of leaven and cutting off of anyone who ate of it was of equal position with the sprinkling the blood. Just as there had to be sprinkling of the blood on the doorframes and eating of the lamb that first night, there also had to be purging of the old leaven. There could be absolutely no leaven in the house with the lamb.[23]

Just as the lamb was central to the Passover meal, bread without leaven was the key to these seven days. But how is that a picture of Christ? In John's gospel, he records what some scholars call the seven 'I Am' statements. The reference to the 'I Am' is from Exodus 3:15 when God clarifies to Moses how he is to identify God to the Israelites. He told Moses "say this to the people of Israel, 'I AM has sent me to you.'"

How does Jesus refer to Himself in John 6:35?

_____

_____

_____

Jesus is the true bread that nourishes us spiritually. Just as God supplied manna in the wilderness to feed His people, Jesus is the bread of life that feeds us in our spiritual walk and provides our eternal life. In the Lord's Supper, the bread represents Christ's body which was sacrificed on the cross for our sins. We see in that same chapter of John's gospel that Jesus said He was the "living bread that came down from heaven" (6:51) and identifies this bread as His flesh, a truth that caused grumbling among the Jews (6:41).

Just as the bread in the feast was _without leaven_, so Christ is the Bread of Life that is _without sin_. We looked last week at New Testament passages that reference Jesus as living a sinless life. Let me suggest to you that just as the manna in the Old Testament was a picture of Jesus as the Bread of Life, the unleavened bread of this feast was also a picture of the Messiah _unleavened_ or without sin. He was the Passover Lamb whose blood was shed so that eternal death could pass over His people and there was no blemish found in Him. Today, Christ dwells within His people and there should be no 'leaven' in the house with the Lamb. We, followers of Christ, are that house and need to say like King David, "Search me, O God, and know my heart! Try me and know my thoughts! And see if there be any grievous way in me and lead me in the way everlasting!" (Psalm 139:23-24).

Day 3 - The Feast of Firstfruits

Well, we have taken a brief look at the first two feasts commanded by God for Israel. The third feast to occur in the religious year was the Feast of Firstfruits. The first four feasts commanded in Leviticus 23 all took place in the spring of the year, with the first three (Passover, Feast of Unleavened Bread and Firstfruits) taking place at the beginning of the cereal grain harvests in Israel. The first of the grains to be harvested in spring was barley which is the grain associated with the Feast of Firstfruits.

The Bible has much to say about first fruits, or first things. God told the people that the "best of the firstfruits of your ground you shall bring into the house of the LORD your God" (Ex 23:19). Concerning firstfruits, Solomon wrote "Honor the LORD with your wealth and with the firstfruits of all you produce" (Prov. 3:9). The giving of the first fruits of whatever they had really implies the *whole* belongs to the Lord. One thing we must remember is that Israel received the land as tenants and understood ownership of the land was the Lord's. They also, in presenting the first and best to Him, acknowledged the benefits from the land were due to God's grace.

The first thing we will do is look at what God said concerning this feast.

Read Leviticus 23:9-14 and complete the following:

The feast would be celebrated when they came _____ the Lord would give them. (v10)

They were to bring the sheaf of the _____ of their harvest to the priest. (v10)

The priest would _____ the sheaf before the _____. (v11)

On the day _____ the Sabbath the priest shall wave the sheaf. (v11)

On the day when the sheaf was waved, they were to offer a _____ (v12)

The lamb was to be one year old without _____ as a _____ offering. (v12)

The grain offering was to be _____ of an ephah of fine flour mixed with oil. (v13)

There were three offerings brought: a _____ offering, a _____ offering (or offering made by fire), and a _____ offering (which represented the grape harvest).

The actual day of this festival was disputed among the Jews. Many, such as the Sadducees (who were the priestly religious party of Jesus' day), believed the phrase "day after the Sabbath" referred to the day after the first weekly Sabbath in the week of the Feast of Unleavened Bread. But since the word *sabbath* could refer to any holy day, many believed the Sabbath day in question was Abib 15, or the first *holy* day of Unleavened Bread. Remember the first and last days of the Feast of Unleavened Bread were to be holy days, observed in a sabbath way. This would mean then that Firstfruits would occur on Abib 16, the day after the holy day. Josephus, a first-century Jewish historian, wrote "But on the second day of unleavened bread, which is the sixteenth day of the month, they first partake of the fruits of the earth, for before that day they do not touch them."[24] The majority belief is that the Passover season was observed as Passover on Abib 14, the Feast of Unleavened Bread begins on Abib 15 and the Feast of Firstfruits on Abib 16.

So on this day, the people were to bring the first sheaf of the new barley crop to the priest who would present it before the Lord. The word *sheaf* in Hebrew is 'omer' which means "measure," with one omer equaling approximately five pints. It was to be brought to the priest from the first and best of the harvest and he would then wave it before God for His acceptance.[25] The priest would actually wave it back and forth for the Lord's acknowledgment of their gratitude for His provision.

The Lord gave instructions to be certain the sheaf brought before Him was the *first*.

> **Write out what God commanded the people concerning eating of the grain from Lev 23:14.**

_____

_____

_____

_____

To assure the offering was the first of the harvest, God commanded that people not eat any of the harvest until this offering was made before Him. It was to be brought with three sacrifices: a burnt offering, a grain offering and a drink offering. For anyone to ignore the commands given concerning the offerings was a very serious offense. In the book written by the prophet Malachi, such an offense was deemed robbery. The prophet wrote "Will man rob God? Yet you are robbing me. But you say, 'How have we robbed you?' In your tithes and contributions. You are cursed with a curse, for you are robbing me, the whole nation of you. Bring the full tithe into the storehouse, that there may be food in my house. And thereby put me to the test, says the LORD of hosts, if I will not open the windows of heaven for you and pour down for you a blessing until there is no more need" Malachi 3:8-10.

The Hebrew word for tithe actually means "a tenth." God promises here that he will provide the rain they need if the people will be faithful to bring their "full tithe." The Lord had designated the tithes and offerings for a specific purpose.

> **Look at Numbers 18:21-24 and note how the offerings were to be used.**

_____

_____

_____

_____

_____

While in the wilderness, the Lord set aside the tribe of Levi for the purpose of serving Him in the Tabernacle. This tribe would not inherit any of the land directly but would be supported by the people through their offerings made to the Lord. From the offerings, God provided for the priests and Levites in return for their service in the tabernacle duties. The Levites were the only tribe that would not receive an inheritance of the land because they were to receive their inheritance from the Lord (or the offerings).

Deut. 18:1-5 *"The Levitical priests, all the tribe of Levi, shall have no portion or inheritance with Israel. They shall eat the Lord's food offerings as their inheritance. They shall have no inheritance among their brothers; the Lord is their inheritance, as he promised them. And this shall be the priests' due from the people, from those offering a sacrifice, whether an ox or a sheep: they shall give to the priest the shoulder and the two cheeks and the stomach. The firstfruits of your grain, of your wine and of your oil, and the first fleece of your sheep, you shall give him. For the Lord your God has chosen him out of all your tribes to stand and minister in the name of the Lord, him and his sons for all time."*

What a privilege it must have been to be a part of the tribe of Levi! First, these men were chosen by God, handpicked to serve Him in the tabernacle. They were not given inheritance from the land, their inheritance was the Lord Himself where they relied solely on God for their provision and literally their survival. They were privileged to receive from Him and serve Him. I truly believe they were a picture of the church at large, for it is our privilege to serve Christ and He is our provision, not only for our eternity but also for our existence now. Peter wrote of this in his first letter concerning our growing in relationship with Christ.

1 Peter 2:4-5 *"As you come to him, a living stone rejected by men but in the sight of God chosen and precious, you yourselves like living stones are being built up as a spiritual house, to be a holy priesthood, to offer spiritual sacrifices acceptable to God through Jesus Christ."*

Believers are to be offering *spiritual* sacrifices, of course, through the power of the Holy Spirit, who is our gift from Jesus Christ. It is the Spirit who teaches and empowers us to live our lives presenting Christ to the world. We are to be like the priest of the Old Testament, serving under the lordship of Jesus Christ.

But the Levites were also required to participate in the offerings, giving the best of what was given to them back to the Lord (Numbers 18:25-28). We see from this that no one was exempt from the tithes and offerings. When the people failed to give their firsts to the Lord, they were robbing Him and also taking away the provisions for the families who provided the temple services. In the New Testament, Paul wrote in support of Christians supporting pastors and church workers for their services just as the Levites had been provided for through the people's offerings.

Galatians 6:6 *"One who is taught the word must share all good things with the one who teaches."*

It is the church's responsibility to support its teachers, which means the pastor and staff who oversee the various congregations. One way this is done is through giving to your local church. If you believe that all you have is from God, giving a portion back to Him should not be a problem or burden, but a joy and desire of your heart.

_____

_____

_____

_____

We have made a pretty good dent in our study of Firstfruits. Tomorrow we will look further, concentrating primarily on what the New Testament records on this subject. Just as with the Passover and Feast of Unleavened Bread, we want to see how the Feast of Firstfruits points to Christ. We will look at that tomorrow. But I want to leave you today with a passage of Scripture that will actually take us into tomorrow's study. When you read the passage below, make a mental note of what God names as His firstfruits.

"We (the priests and people) obligate ourselves to bring the firstfruits of our ground and the firstfruits of all fruit of every tree, year by year, to the house of the LORD, also to bring to the house of our God, to the priests who minister in the house of our God, the firstborn of our sons and of our cattle, as it its written in the Law, and the firstborn of our herds and of our flocks; and to bring the first of our dough, and our contributions, the fruit of every tree, the wine and the oil, to the priests, to the chambers of the house of our God; and to bring to the Levites the tithes from our ground, for it is the Levites who collect the tithes in all our towns where we labor. And the priest, the son of Aaron, shall be with the Levites when the Levites receive the tithes. And the Levites shall bring up the tithe of the tithes to the house of our God, to the chambers of the storehouse. For the people of Israel and the sons of Levi shall bring the contribution of grain, wine, and oil to the chambers where the vessels of the sanctuary are, as well as the priests who minister, and the gatekeepers and the singers. We will not neglect the house of our God" (Nehemiah 10:35-39).

Day 4 - God First

All that we have belongs to the Lord. That really is the message of Firstfruits. Maybe one way to look at it is all is given to us on loan by God. We are to be good stewards, using the whole to glorify Him. The Feast of Firstfruits is the festival which acknowledges that all is the Lord's. It could be considered a day of thanksgiving to the Lord, publicly confessing His grace and mercy.

Yesterday we looked at the commands concerning the waving of the sheaf on the day of Firstfruits (Abib 16), which was a measure of barley. But the passage we ended with from Nehemiah confirmed that grain and flock were not the only things God considered *firstfruits*.

_____

_____

_____

_____

Nehemiah restates the offerings required from the field and flock but also notes additional firstfruits we have not studied. The people were to bring not only the grain but the first of their dough in the form of a loaf (cf. Numbers 15:20). Firstfruits were to include grain, animals, dough, wine, oil, and fruit, all to be used to support those who maintain the house of God.

There was one other firstfruit mentioned in this passage, the firstborn sons. Remember the blood of the Passover lamb was placed on the doorframes to save the life of the firstborn son and cattle in Egypt. Everything belongs to the Lord, even children. But how did this work, since only the Levites served the tabernacle? Did the Israelites have to bring their firstborn sons and deliver them over to the priests? We need to look at what Scripture says concerning the firstfruits of sons.

In Jeremiah 2:3, what is the first fruit?

_____

_____

_____

_____

Jeremiah documents God's laments over Israel's spiritual adultery. Here God reminds the people of how He gave them the land and of their devotion to Him in that time. He calls them "the firstfruits of His harvest" because He chose them to be His people out of all the nations. Israel was set apart to be a blessing to God and to be used to bless the world. Israel was holy because they had been set apart from the other nations as God's firstfruit for His purpose, to be His people. Just as they were to bring the best of their possessions, they were to present themselves to Him living lives that glorified Him.

Look at Exodus 13:2 and note what God states concerning firstborn?

_____

_____

_____

_____

That is not hard to understand. Israel was to *consecrate* all the firstborn to the Lord. Of course, to *consecrate* is to dedicate it to God. They are "set apart for the service of God. The Hebrew *qadesh* and Greek *hagiazo* are translated by several different English words: holy, consecrate, hallow, sanctify, dedicate."[26] Though the firstborn of the flock, with the exception of donkeys, were to be sacrificed, God offered redemption for the firstborn sons.

> **Read in Exodus 13:12-15. What does God say about sons?**

_____

_____

_____

_____

Just as in Egypt, the blood of a lamb was the redemption for the firstborn sons in the Promised Land. The people would offer a lamb to free their sons from lifetime service. In Numbers, it is explained that "the firstborn of man you shall redeem, and the firstborn of unclean animals you shall redeem. And their redemption price (at a month old you shall redeem them) you shall fix at five shekels in silver. . ." (Num 18:15b-16a). Walter Kaiser, Jr., explains "the firstborn were owned by the LORD; for he dramatically spared them in the tenth plague, and he had previously called them to be his firstborn."[27] The Lord stated "for all the firstborn are mine. On the day that I struck down all the firstborn in the land of Egypt, I consecrated for my own all the firstborn in Israel, both of man and of beast. They shall be mine: I am the Lord" (Numbers 3:13).

Jesus was the firstborn son of Mary, so according to the Law, Mary and Joseph brought him to the Temple for his *Pidyon Haben*, or dedication ceremony. Pidyon Haben means "redemption of the son" in Hebrew.[28] Luke records the account of Jesus being brought because it was written in the Law (see Luke 2:23a). The Law also spoke of the requirements for cleansing of the mother after childbirth. The Bible records a couple of occasions where Mary and Joseph honor the Lord by keeping the Law. Though Jesus was to be *the* Redeemer, he was still presented for redemption before the priest as the Law dictated.

> **Write out what Luke 2:23 says firstborns are to be called.**

_____

_____

_____

_____

Of course, Luke was quoting from the Old Testament Law which states the firstborn male is "holy to the Lord." Luke continues in this passage to record how the infant Jesus is identified by Simeon and then the prophetess Anna as the Lord's Christ. So it is with the offering for the firstborn (or firstfruit) that Jesus is first declared the Messiah. But not only was there a firstfruit offering made for the Messiah, He Himself is the fulfillment of the Feast of Firstfruits. Just like the Feasts of Passover and Unleavened Bread, the Feast of Firstfruits finds its prophetic fulfillment in the first coming of Christ.

> **Note what Paul states concerning firstfruits in 1 Corinthians 15:20.**

_____

_____

_____

_____

After reading that verse, some may be thinking 'what about Lazarus and the ruler's daughter, both of whom Jesus raised up from the dead? How can He be the firstfruit of those who have died?' Well, because those before Him who were raised from the dead eventually died again, but He rose and then ascended to the right hand of God.

With His resurrection from the dead, Jesus became our firstfruit. On the third day of Passover Jesus rose from the dead. Just as the first three feasts of the spring season occurred consecutively over three days, the Messiah's death, burial and resurrection also occurred in three days—the exact days of these feasts. He was crucified on Passover, was in the grave for Unleavened Bread and rose on the day of Firstfruits. "The resurrection of Jesus is the guarantee and the beginning (firstfruits) of the final harvest, or resurrection, of all mankind. The Messiah fulfilled the prophetic meaning of this holy day by rising from the dead to become the firstfruits of the resurrection, and He did it on the very day of Firstfruits."[29]

Even in the Old Testament we are assured that there is life after death. But what kind of life is determined by our choice in this life, Christ or Satan. "And many of those who sleep in the dust of the earth shall awake, some to everlasting life, some to shame and everlasting contempt" (Daniel 12:2). For some, their inheritance will be to dwell with the Lord, but for others their inheritance will be eternal separation from God. But for everyone, there will be an eternity.

> **Read James 1:18 and note what is written concerning firstfruit.**

_____

_____

_____

According to Grant Osborne in the ESV Study Bible, James speaks of spiritual salvation. He is talking of believers saved through the gospel. Believers are "brought . . . forth" as in from the womb, which is a metaphor for the new birth.[30] Being a Jew, James understood the whole harvest followed the sheaf offering waved before the Lord. In the same way, Christians are the firstfruit before the Lord from which will come the greater harvest. On the morning of Abib 16 (or Nisan 16 as it was known in the New Testament), the Jews awoke to the Feast of Firstfruits. On that Sunday following the Passover feast and first day of Unleavened Bread, they awoke to the true Firstfruit of the Lord, which was Jesus Christ.

I wonder if the disciples and the women at the grave that morning put it all together. If once they found He had risen from the dead, did they understand the first three of the feasts were fulfilled? It was the morning of the Feast of Firstfruits, the Paschal lamb had been sacrificed, all leaven had been removed, and the people were preparing to take the sheaf to the priests to be waved before the Lord. Yet God had delivered His *true firstfruit* from death that very morning.

The fact Jesus' death and resurrection took place on the same three days as the Feasts of Passover, Unleavened Bread and Firstfruits was no coincidence. It was God's plan from the beginning. When He gave Moses the instructions for each of these feasts hundreds of years before, God was explaining His Son's death, burial and resurrection. Don't you love this? How can anyone study this and not believe! I just do not believe that men could put this all together.

Our study really just brushes the surface of what Scripture tells us about the first three annual feasts of Israel and their fulfillment in Christ. But you can be certain all point to Jesus as the Lamb, the True Bread and the Firstfruit. My prayer for each one who reads this is that you will grow in your understanding of God's truth and will grow more in love with His Word.

Next week we will look at the Feast of Weeks, the feast celebrated fifty days after Firstfruits. I hope you are looking forward to it, I know I am.

Week 3 - **The Feast of Weeks**

Day 1 - Shavuot

Our third week has us looking at the fourth feast mentioned in Leviticus 23, known in the Old Testament as the Feast of Weeks. We have already noted that the first three feasts were celebrated on consecutive days in the spring and are often referenced as one feast in Scripture. The Feast of Weeks is the final feast to occur in the spring season.

The word *weeks* in Hebrew is 'Shavuot' (or shabuwa), with Hag Ha*shavuot* meaning Feast of Weeks.[31] It is the fourth of Israel's holy days and the second of the three pilgrimage feasts when Jewish men had to travel to a specified location, which later was Jerusalem (the other two being the Feast of Unleavened Bread and the Feast of Tabernacles.) Just as the Feast of Firstfruits marked the beginning of the barley harvest, this feast marked the beginning of the summer wheat harvest. The Feast of Weeks is sometimes referenced by a different name.

> **Read Exodus 23:16a and note the name.**

_____

_____

_____

_____

This feast was also known as the Feast of Harvest, with the Feast of Ingathering another name for the Feast of Tabernacles, which is the last of the annual feasts. The Feast of Harvest represented the beginning of the summer harvest of wheat. That certainly makes sense, but why was it also called the Feast of *Weeks* when it was only a *one day* feast?

The Israelites were to:

Count off _____ weeks (23:15b).

Count off _____ days up to the day after the _____ Sabbath, (23:16a) then present a _____ to the Lord (16b).

From where they lived they were to bring _____ loaves made of fine flour, baked with _____, as firstfruits to the Lord (23:17).

Present with this bread _____ a year old and without _____, _____ bull and _____ rams (23:18a).

They were a _____ offering to the Lord along with their grain and drink offerings (23:18).

Sacrifice one male goat for a _____ offering and two lambs, each a year old, as _____ offerings (23:19).

The priest was to _____ the two lambs before the Lord together with the _____ of the firstfruits (23:20a).

On that same day they were to hold a _____ and do no _____ work (23:21a).

This was an eternal statute for the generations to come (23:21b).

The Feast of Weeks was a one-day feast that would occur fifty days after the Feast of Firstfruits. In the ESV Study Bible, the passage reads "count seven full weeks from the day after the Sabbath, from the day that you brought the sheaf of the wave offering. You shall count *fifty days* to the day after the seventh Sabbath. . ." (23:15-16a, emphasis added). Remember that the *sheaf of the wave offering* was presented on the day of Firstfruits, which was the day *after the Sabbath* of Unleavened Bread. They were to count fifty days, or seven weeks and a day, from that offering to arrive at the Feast of Weeks. So this feast was actually tied to the Passover week because its date was determined by calculating from the Feast of Firstfruits, which again was part of Passover week. The weeks counted were those between the barley harvest (Feast of Firstfruits) and the wheat harvest.

Look at how exact God is in His instructions to His people. Keep in mind the Israelites did not have calendars prepared for them years ahead as we do today, so it was necessary for God to give these specifics in order for them to get the day right. This day was to be a *holy* day, celebrated as a Sabbath, set aside for God in which there was to be no regular work, so it was very important that they get the right day. The Lord helped them with this, as he always does give us everything we need.

On this day the people were to offer up as burnt offerings to the Lord seven one year old lambs, one bull and two rams. A male goat was offered for a sin offering and two one year old male lambs were offered as peace offerings. With these the people were to bring two loaves of bread made with grain from the harvest. All of these offerings symbolized the people's understanding that *all* they had was from God and He deserved to receive the first of the harvest, whether grain, fruit or animal.

Something we have not looked at but need to have a general understanding of is the various offerings. In this passage a number of different offerings were required: burnt offering, peace offering, grain offering, sin offering, and wave offering.

> **Think back to last week's study of Firstfruits and write down an explanation of the wave offering.**

_____

_____

_____

In our study of the Feast of Firstfruits, we saw that the **wave offering** was when the priest took the sheaf or bundle of grain from the harvest and literally waved it before the Lord as a means of celebrating the harvest given by God. With the Feast of Weeks, the priest would wave two loaves of bread *and* two lambs.

The **burnt offering** (Lev 1:1-17) was the one offering that was completely burned up, leaving nothing except the skin of the animal. It was always to be a male without blemish, or the best of the flock and could be a lamb, goat, turtledove, bull or even a pigeon. The one giving the animal was to place his hand on the animal's head, probably symbolizing that the animal was a substitute given on his behalf (Lev 1:4). According to this same verse, the animal was *to make atonement for* the one giving it. Blood of the animal was to be thrown on the altar by the priest (God's representative) and then the animal was to be burnt completely there on the altar. It was to be a *pleasing* aroma to the Lord, which implies the Lord welcomed it or considered the offering to be acceptable.

The **peace offering** (explained in Leviticus 3) is similar to the burnt offering except only the fat and certain organs of the animal were burned on the altar. The people of ancient Israel considered the fat of the animal to be the best of it. It symbolized that God is worthy of their best and suggested a peace between the person bringing the offering and God. The Lord had commanded that all fat was His and that the people were not to eat any fat or blood (Lev 3:16-17). This offering could be presented as an offering of thanksgiving, a vow, or a freewill offering (Lev 7:11-21). According to the ESV Study Bible notes, this offering represented a communion meal observed by the offerer, the priest and the Lord. These meals were often observed when affirming a covenant or agreement where all the parties involved would partake. This would suggest that the offering was given as a reminder of the covenant between God and Israel.[32]

A **sin offering** (instructed in Leviticus 4) was one offered to make amends for going against one of God's commands, even unintentionally (Lev 4:2). This offering was usually dependent on the offense and/or position of the person involved (i.e., priest, elder, congregation, etc.) and was a purifying offering. The animals offered would be a bull for a priest or the congregation, a male goat for a leader, and a female goat or lamb for an individual. Specific instructions are given for the slaughtering of the animals, where it was to be offered, the use of the blood, and how they were to dispose of the remaining animal parts. In Leviticus 5, Moses documents the Lord's requirements concerning the **guilt offerings**. Though this seems to be just like the sin offering, the guilt offering actually dealt with more serious offenses. They also seem to be more costly for the individual because a male animal is required rather than a female.

The **grain offering** is commanded in Leviticus 2 and 6 requiring the people to bring grain as fine flour mixed with oil and frankincense to the priest who would burn a handful of it on the altar. The remainder of the offering was to be for the priests' use because it was "a most holy part of the Lord's food offerings" (Lev. 2:3b). Remember, some of the offerings brought to the Lord were used to support the priests and their families. This was one of those offerings. It was also the only offering that did not require the shedding of blood.

I know that was probably a lot of information but it was helpful for me to get an understanding of the various offerings and hopefully you found it helpful as well. I really think we needed to take a brief look at all the possible offerings/sacrifices. It is one of those things that we normally tend to skip. Tomorrow, we will take a closer look at some of the specifics of the fourth feast.

Day 2 - Lord of the Harvest

The Feast of Weeks was a dedication of the wheat harvest to the Lord. Both the barley and wheat harvests were considered a sign of the land's fruitfulness and God's provision for Israel.

Read Deuteronomy 8: 1-10 and record what the Lord promised about the land.

_____

_____

_____

The people were still in the wilderness when they received this word from the Lord. It was a time when their diet consisted of manna and quail every day. But God described the land as being a place where they would *lack nothing* (8:9). These had to be very precious words to the Israelites. He assured them just before entering the Promised Land that it would provide figs, grapes, olives, pomegranates along with barley and wheat. They were promised that they would *eat and be full* but also that they were to *bless* the Lord because He was the provider of all they would receive in the good land. Israel understood who was responsible for their harvests.

Just as a side bar, notice how Moses described the wilderness years in the above passage. Originally, the people were made to wander forty years because of their unbelief in God's ability to give them the land. They feared the inhabitants they saw more than they believed God and so received a year for every day the spies spent in the land.

What does Moses say the Lord used the years in the wilderness to reveal (8:2)?

_____

_____

_____

Their wilderness wandering time was meant to reveal the condition of their hearts. But it was not for the Lord's benefit, for certainly He knew the hearts of His people. No, it was for the people to see their own heart condition. It was also during that time when God showed Israel what a powerful God they served. One who could supply heavenly bread, keep clothing from wearing out, and keep tired feet from swelling. Seriously, not having feet swell must have been awesome for any pregnant woman during those years. All of this should have let the people see that what they needed was God.

Psalm 147 is one of the great writings in Scripture that talk of the Creator's provision and care for His creation, especially His chosen Israel.

Look at Psalm 147:10-14 and write out all you learn about the Lord.

_____

_____

_____

The Lord is the strength of our gates, the one who blesses our children and He is the one who makes peace within our borders and gives the finest wheat to His people. I love that, He does not simply provide any wheat but the _finest_ wheat. Well, He is the one who created it so of course His is the best.

This is such a great Psalm for several reasons, one in particular is that it starts and finishes with the same statement—Praise the Lord! That is what the day of Shavout was about, praising God for the harvest. It was a day of thanksgiving. The passage in Psalm 147 also explains that He does not take pleasure in strength exhibited by animals or men but in those who fear Him and put their hope in His love. His is a steadfast love, a love that is true and constant, one that endures because it is persistent. Throughout the Old Testament the Lord is described as having a steadfast love for His own (Gen. 39:21, Ex.15:13, Ex. 34:6, Deut. 7:9). That steadfast love was shown in many ways but one was in the provision of the harvests, for which He certainly should be praised.

In yesterday's study when you were filling in the instructions given to the people concerning the feast, part of the people's praise was in the form of a wave offering. They were to bring two loaves of bread made with the grain of their harvest to the priest, who would wave the loaves along with the two male lambs before God. But did you notice anything different about the two loaves of bread that were to be offered as a wave offering to the Lord?

_____

_____

_____

_____

The passage states the Israelites were to bring the two loaves of bread from their dwelling places. The Holman CSB translates this "from your settlements," with the King James Version as "out of your habitations." This may have been because the Feast of Weeks was one of the feasts that would later require all Jewish men to appear before the Lord (Deut 16:16). But where were they to appear? It was to be the place of God's choosing, which would ultimately be the city of Jerusalem. During the wilderness years and prior to Solomon's temple, it was wherever the Tabernacle was erected. I believe the key is that they were to go to God, where He had established His dwelling among the people.

The two loaves were to be baked from fine flour and _with_ leaven. Remember from day two of last week's study we saw that the way dough was leavened was by adding starter dough to new ingredients. This would link the two batches of bread and, in this case, probably the two crops. The Lord commanded that the people could not eat of the harvest until the offering was presented before Him, so when the two loaves are prepared no bread has been made with wheat, only the grain from the previous crops, which was barley. Barley was the crop of the Feast of Firstfruits, which was the third day of Passover week. So I am thinking if the bread was leavened using starter dough, the starter dough would have been from the barley harvest and would, in a sense, connect the two crops as well as the two feasts.

The Feasts of Firstfruits and Weeks were connected by the countdown from one to the other, but also possibly by the bread. While studying the feasts one book that I really enjoyed is Christ in the Feast of Pentecost by David Brickner and Rich Robinson (and I highly recommend). They make the point that in connecting the two feasts, God's people would recognize that, even in a land surrounded by pagan nations, everything good was by the hand of the same one who delivered them from the bondage of Egypt.[33] Jehovah God was the only God, not the Egyptian gods or the Canaanite gods. And it was Israel's God who was to be praised and worshiped for their harvests.

Still we also saw last week that leaven often represented sin in Scripture. According to Kevin L. Howard, these bread offerings were unique because they were made with leaven, and for this reason they could not be burned upon the brazen altar. God had given Moses specific instructions not to burn anything with leaven or honey in any burnt offering to the Lord (Lev 2:11). These loaves and the peace offering of lambs were presented to God as wave offerings by the priests, then eaten as part of the priests' festival meal, but since the bread was not offered on the altar they could be made with leaven.

Yet it does make you pause a bit, doesn't it? The people had observed the seven days of Unleavened Bread when all leaven was purged from their homes and territories. There was no leaven served with the Passover Lamb. Now, seven weeks later, leaven _was_ presented in the bread given to the priests. I don't know that we are told exactly why leaven was to be included but many have speculated. One thought that seems reasonable is that "the presence of leaven in the two loaves may be a statement that even the fruit of our labors is tainted by sin; or it may simply represent that God wanted not only the raw materials but the product prepared by human hands. . . Until our redemption (and our sanctification) is complete, even our best efforts are less than perfect and may be tainted by sin."[34] These loaves were made by the offerer (or sinner) so they were not going to be perfect. Just like the loaves, we offer up our lives and efforts everyday to our God and they are not perfect. The same holds true today of our *offerings* to (or efforts for) God, they are less than perfect. Yet we have a Savior who speaks for us stating that we have His blood to make up for our imperfect offering. The apostle John explained "But if anyone does sin, we have an advocate with the Father, Jesus Christ, the righteous" (1 John 2:1).

It amazes me the lengths God goes to in order to show who He is and what He is about. He is all about having a loving relationship with us, giving us every opportunity to be His children. And yes, He was doing that even in the feasts. Come on, these were days throughout the year set aside to focus just on Him and all He was doing for Israel, days that would continually draw the people back to God. The Feast of Weeks was just such a day reminding the people that God was their provision. And those two loaves of bread with leaven, I think, were possibly His way of saying to the people 'I love you anyway.' That is mind boggling!

I really believe we have gotten a good start on this feast but we still have plenty to look at concerning it. Don't give out on me now, hang in there.

Day 3 - Honoring His Word

The Feast of Weeks, or Shavout, was the fourth of Israel's annual feasts and marked the end of the Passover season. There were several offerings involved with this feast including the waving of the grain offering, yet there does seem to be one thing that is not mentioned with this one—what event does it commemorate? The Feast of Weeks was one of the three pilgrimage feasts and the only one that seems to have no prior event in Israel's history which it memorializes. But is that really true?

According to later Jewish tradition, the day of the Festival of Weeks was believed to have been established on the same day Moses was given the Law at Mount Sinai. After the Romans destroyed the Temple and Jerusalem in A.D. 70, the Jewish people no longer had a central place for worship or the offering of sacrifices. It is believed that at that time their primary occupation was no longer to farm the land, which meant harvest was not central to them as a people any longer. The Jewish religious council of that era decided to make the giving of the Law at Mt. Sinai the event commemorated by this feast. Some believe Moses makes this connection in Deuteronomy 16:12.

Read Deuteronomy 16:12 and note what it says concerning the Feast of Weeks.

_____

_____

_____

The book of Deuteronomy is considered the second giving of the Law to Israel's second generation by Moses before they entered the Promised Land. Moses restates the statutes of God to the people which included restating the feast requirements. In this passage, Moses reminds the people of their time in Egypt. As with Passover, they were to remember Israel's time of slavery in Egypt and God's deliverance with the celebrating of this feast. This instruction seems to tie the first four feasts together.

But I have to admit I am a little baffled by the choice of Deuteronomy 16:12 by some as proof to connect the Feast of Weeks with the giving of the Law. Understand I am not questioning if these two occurred in the same season. I believe the Jewish tradition of the Feast of Weeks falling on the same day the Law was given has merit. The passage in Deuteronomy 16 speaking to the giving of the Law is what confuses me. And I mention this to warn you that we need to test what is explained about Scripture in other books, commentaries, podcasts, or sermons. Keep in mind that the best teacher of Scripture is always Scripture itself. I do think the Old Testament, though it may not state it explicitly, does suggest the time frame the Law was given and that it corresponds with the Feast of Weeks.

> **What does Exodus 19:1 say concerning the time span from Israel's exodus until Mt Sinai?**

_____

_____

_____

This passage states that it was the *third new moon* after the people of Israel had left Egypt when they came to Mount Sinai. Now, I am no scientist. The reality is I do not really care for science as a subject and never excelled at it. But, for the sake of this feast, I am going to give you some general information that may help. An average lunar month is 29 or 30 days and Israel came to Mt Sinai at the third. If the first occurred during or on Passover, it would coincide with the seven weeks required between the Feast of Firstfruits and the Feast of Weeks. Some may not believe we can know for certain that this feast and the giving of the Law coincide because the Bible does not spell it out for us. I think it does give enough evidence.

But what it does absolutely tell us is when they participated in this feast, they were to remember Israel's time of slavery. The fact that it comes at the time of the wheat harvest emphasizes the theme of God's provision and of the gratitude that should be shown to Him.

I found this portion very interesting because I have often been curious as to how the Jewish people continue to celebrate the feasts when they no longer have a Temple, altar or really the means to offer the sacrifices. The truth is there is no longer a need for the sacrifices because Jesus Christ provided the best and final sacrifice. However, the Jews as a whole do not accept that Jesus is the Messiah so they are a sacrificial religion without a means of sacrifice. Because of this fact, I have been (and I think some of you as well) curious as to what they do with their feasts that call for offerings. With Passover, the meal has been adapted but the focus is still on the lamb and remembering what God did for His people. Counting the days between the Feast of Firstfruits and the Feast of Weeks is really the only ritual acknowledged by some Jews today for Firstfruits. Others may combine Firstfruits and the Feast of Weeks, celebrating the height of the grain and fruit harvests. This would include wheat, barley, grapes, figs, and honey (as noted in Deuteronomy 8:8).

With Shavuot, the decision to commemorate the giving of the Law was quickly accepted and this feast became a celebration of the original birth of the Jewish nation. It became known as Zeman Mattan Toratenu, or 'the time of the giving of our Law.'[35] But the people did not forget that this was a feast concerned with the harvest and God's provision. Most synagogues and homes are decorated with flowers and greenery to emphasize the fact that it is a harvest festival and includes special food such as bread, dairy and sweet foods. The dairy and sweets may be in reference to Exodus 3:8b and the description of the land being a land *flowing with milk and honey,* while the bread is certainly in respect to God's instruction to offer two loaves of bread.

Different Old Testament passages are read and observant Jews will stay up *all night* studying and discussing the Torah (yes, all night). Jewish folklore tells of the people oversleeping on the day Moses returned from the mountain at Sinai and Moses had to wake them to give them the Law. Many believe the tradition of staying awake studying the Word is to make up for the people's failure to remain awake centuries earlier. Whatever the reason, I still think it is amazing they do that, but knowing and understanding God's Word is certainly worthy of an all-night study.

Some will study the "opening and closing verses of each Sabbath reading, the opening and closing verses of each book of the Bible, and the entire Book of Ruth."[36] Those in Jerusalem will go to the site of the ancient Temple at dawn into the Western Wall plaza and recite the ancient Amidah prayer. "The Amidah or 'standing' prayer with its nineteen blessings dates back more than 2,000 years. It forms the central prayer of all prayer services-morning, afternoon, evening, Sabbath and holidays."[37] Are you as amazed as I am that these people are willing to stay up all night studying the Bible?! Goodness, we sometimes get annoyed when our worship service runs a little longer that an hour.

Besides the studying of the opening and closing verses of each book of the Bible, there were some passages from the Old Testament that received special attention and were read in the synagogue to the congregation. These passages were Ezekiel 1:1-28, 3:12; Habakkuk 2:20-3:19, Exodus 19-20 and the book of Ruth. The passage in Ezekiel describes God's glory and in Habakkuk is the prophet's prayer addressing God's wrath, mercy and strength. The chapters in Exodus were included once the festival focused on the giving of the Law. And, finally, the book of Ruth is read and that is where we want to focus the remainder of today.

Don't get me wrong, the other passages are also important and I encourage each of you to read through them. For this study we are going to only look at Ruth and why this book is read in connection with the Feast of Weeks.

The book of Ruth is about a Moabite widow of a Jewish man, whose mother-in-law was named Naomi. The book is based during the time of the Judges and provides important information concerning Israel's history. From this book, we learn the story of King David's ancestors and God's providence over David's inclusion in the messianic and monarchical lines. Ruth eventually met and married Boaz, later becoming the great-grandparents of David. Ruth's story is also an excellent demonstration of the law concerning the Kinsman Redeemer (Deuteronomy 25:5). Boaz is a picture of the believer's relationship with Christ, and in this story we see "how Christ, our Kinsman Redeemer, purchases us for Himself. It also illustrates the grace of God as Ruth the Gentile is brought into the line of messianic blessing."[38] But why read it in connection with the celebration of the Feast of Weeks?

The story of Ruth takes place during the barley harvest (Ruth 1:22b), which occurred just weeks before the wheat harvest began and would have been during the weeks counting down until Shavuot. Another reason this story is key is because of how Boaz's faithfulness to God's instructions concerning harvesting and the poor.

> **Read Leviticus 23:22 and write out what God instructed concerning the poor.**

Boaz did not harvest the full span of his fields but left the edges along with the gleanings, or droppings, of his men for the poor. Now notice God did not say they were to gather these portions up and take or give them to the poor. The poor had to work for this portion, but it was by God's grace and Boaz's obedience that Ruth could harvest barley in order for she and her mother-in-law to have food to eat. Boaz was obedient to God's instructions. Mercy shown to others revealed his heart but also his gratitude to the Lord, because he obviously understood he was simply the steward of what God had given him.

That is what the Feast of Weeks is about; recognizing that what we have is by God's grace and provision. But it is also about the relationship of man-to-man, or being concerned for others. We need to be good stewards of what God has provided for each of us and willingly use that for His glory, which would include helping other people. Here again we see the Lord providing Israel with teachable moments for themselves and their children. With Passover, He stated that when their children asked questions about the feast, they were to teach them about what God had done for them. The same holds true with this feast and providing for the poor. This was an opportunity to not only remember how great God is, but also to instruct the children of giving to others because He had provided for them, not being selfish, and loving God enough to honor His Word.

We have one more day of looking at the Feast of Weeks and it has to be my favorite day of this week. Tomorrow we will see the New Testament fulfillment of this festival. I have to admit it has been difficult for me not to go straight to day four. I cannot wait to get to it and hope you feel the same way.

Day 4 - The Coming of His Spirit

We are going to end our study on the Feast of Weeks in the New Testament. We know that the feast was a one day festival whose name indicates *counting* because they were to count fifty days (or seven weeks and a day) from the Feast of Firstfruits for its occurrence. The name used for this festival in the New Testament also suggests counting.

Read Acts 2:1. What *day* is mentioned in this passage?

_____

_____

_____

It was the *day of Pentecost* and Christ's followers were *all together in one place*. The word Pentecost is the Greek word meaning *fiftieth*. Pentecost is the word used to refer to this feast in the Septuagint, which is the Greek translation of the Old Testament, and became the way the New Testament Jews referenced the festival. Even in the Greek, the name gives reference to the *counting* involved with this feast. And whether it is seven weeks and one day or fifty days, they would arrive at the same end.

For the New Testament church, the day of Pentecost was very important. Remember Jesus was with His followers for forty days after His resurrection and before ascending to heaven. But before leaving, He had promised them something.

Let's look at Jesus' final instructions to His disciples by reading Luke 24:44-49 and fill in the following:

Everything must be _____ that is written about _____ in the Law of Moses, the Prophets and the Psalms (24:44).

Then He _____ their minds so they could _____ the Scriptures (24:45).

He told them ". . . it is written, that the Christ should _____ and on the third day _____ from the dead, (24:46) and that _____ and _____ of sins should be proclaimed in his name to all _____ , beginning from Jerusalem (24:47)."

According to Luke 24:49, what was Jesus sending to the disciples?

_____

_____

_____

Jesus was speaking to the disciples about things He had already told them prior to His crucifixion (see Luke 9:21-22). He references the Old Testament scriptures as the Law of Moses, the Prophets and the Psalms. And He makes it very clear that the Old Testament is all about Him and the events of their last forty days were all the fulfillment of Scripture.

A large part of the fulfillment He spoke of had already taken place with His death, burial and resurrection. He may have even explained how these were the fulfillment of the first three feasts (Passover, Unleavened Bread and Firstfruits). But in His teaching He promises that He will send *the promise of the Father upon you* (24:49a). He is, of course, referring to the Holy Spirit, of whom John the Baptist had prophesied at the time of Jesus' baptism. John stated ". . . he who is mightier than I is coming, the strap of whose sandals I am not worthy to untie. He will baptize you with the Holy Spirit *and* with fire" (Luke 3:16, emphasis added). John tells the people that the baptism of the Holy Spirit will be proof of Christ's coming.

Jesus told the disciples that He was sending the Holy Spirit to them and they were to remain in Jerusalem and wait until that time. Luke tells us that at His ascension ". . . they worshiped him and returned to Jerusalem with great joy, and were continually in the temple blessing God" (Luke 24:52-53). They were excited at the prospect of His promise, were expecting or trusting in its fulfillment, and obedient to His instruction to remain in Jerusalem. This is a very different group of people from the way they were prior to His resurrection. Remember these are the same people who were huddled up together in the upper room in fear with the doors bolted. Here they are worshiping openly in the Temple among the same Sanhedrin leaders responsible for their Master's death.

So why were they so different? What happened to the fearful group? Well, certainly seeing their Lord alive was huge in bringing about this change. They had just spent forty days with Him and had seen Him ascend into heaven back to the Father. It had to have made an impact on their hearts and souls. But I believe Luke shares one other tidbit that would offer an additional explanation.

What did Jesus do for them according to Luke 24:45?

_____

_____

_____

Just as He had done with the pair on the road to Emmaus, Jesus *opened their minds to understand the Scriptures*. This understanding is a gift of complete understanding and is one only God can give. Earlier in His ministry, Jesus spoke to the disciples about being "delivered into the hands of men" but they did not understand what He was saying because "it was concealed from them" (Luke 9:44-45). An almost identical statement is recorded later in Luke's gospel. "But they understood none of these things. This saying was hidden from them, and they did not grasp what was said" (Luke 18:34). The disciples all spoke the same language, so they understood what He was telling them but they did not understand the why of God's plan. Their confusion was primarily with the fact that He had to die on a cross and resurrect from the dead on the third day. It is God who gives us understanding of His Word. So, just prior to the Feast of Weeks or Pentecost, Jesus opened the minds of the disciples so they could understand the Scriptures and would be waiting for the Spirit to come to them in a little more than a week. The Helper, as Jesus called Him earlier is His ministry, was going to teach the disciples and bring remembrance to them of all Jesus had said to them (John 14:26). Jesus did not leave his disciples unaware, but prepared them for the coming of His Spirit.

John 16:13-14 *"When the Spirit of truth comes, he will guide you into all the truth, for he will not speak on his own authority, but whatever he hears he will speak, and he will declare to you the things that are to come. He will glorify me, for he will take what is mine and declare it to you."*

The Spirit was a gift to Christ's believers to teach and guide them to glorify Christ. Like Jesus, He only speaks what He hears from the Father, so He speaks only truth. No wonder the disciples were a calm and probably excited group. They were waiting for the gifting of the one, the promised one, who would enable them in all they would endeavor for their Lord.

In the Old Testament, Pentecost was a festival honoring the harvest given to the people by God. I want to submit to you that in the New Testament it would be nothing less than a harvest given by God. Pentecost was a one-day feast held in Jerusalem. Thousands of Jewish men and probably their families would have been at the Temple on this day of rest to focus on Jehovah God. And it was this day that God had planned for thousands of years to gift His believers with the Holy Spirit and bring about a harvest of souls for His church. It was on this day that God chose to birth His Church. That is so amazing and so God!

Let's look further at the New Testament account of Pentecost given by Luke in Acts 2.

Look again at Acts 2:1-8.

There would have been thousands of Jews, both pilgrims and residents, in Jerusalem for the Feast of Weeks, or the day of Pentecost, probably expecting to hear readings from the books of Ezekiel and Habakkuk. What they did not expect was the sudden sound like *a mighty, rushing wind* that came from heaven and filled the house where Jesus' followers were staying. But notice in verse six that the multitude also heard the sound and gathered together in the area where the disciples were staying. So it is very possible that the upper room was very close to the temple grounds.

The crowd was drawn by the sound from heaven but confused by what they encountered. They heard the disciples speaking in *other tongues* as enabled by the Holy Spirit (Acts 2:4). Here they are, men from every nation and various languages hearing the disciples speak in such a way so everyone present could completely understand what was being said. I cannot begin to understand this much less explain it except to say it was the power of the Spirit of God.

They saw what seemed to be _____ of _____ that appeared and came to rest on each of them (2:3).

All of them were _____ with the _____ _____ (2:4).

They began to speak in other _____ as the Spirit *gave them utterance* (2:4).

Here we have the fulfillment of Jesus' promise, when the Holy Spirit came to God's people in a new and very powerful way. The Spirit of God came upon each one of Christ's followers and enabled them to either speak in different languages or be understood in different languages. The word for *tongues* used here in the Greek is 'glossa' which is plural and can be translated *languages,* suggesting that this was a speaking miracle where they all spoke outside of their personal ability. That it was outside their natural ability was obvious to the crowd because the men speaking were noticeably Galilean. Galileans were not known to be educated men, so they would not be expected to speak in so many different languages. Also what they were saying was very distinctive, they were telling of the *mighty works of God* (2:11).

Now to see something else astounding, we need to go to Ezekiel to look at one of the customary readings for Pentecost?

Look at Ezekiel 1:4 and make note of anything that you notice that might have given the people pause on that day in Acts 2:

_____

_____

_____

Ezekiel 1:4 speaks of a stormy wind from the north, a great cloud, and fire flashing. It is very possible that the people who were privileged enough to witness all that took place that day may have wondered if what they were seeing had anything to do with what they heard from the prophet Ezekiel (remember they asked "what does this mean? Acts 2:12). Ezekiel also wrote of the glory of God leaving the Temple and ascending into heaven before the Temple's destruction by Babylon (Ezekiel 10). Maybe they wondered if God's glory was going to return to the Temple. Of course, His glory had been in the Temple every time Jesus had entered it, but sadly few if any understood.

In the Old Testament, it was common for wind to be present with an appearance of God. The prophet Isaiah wrote "For behold, the LORD will come in fire, and his chariots like the whirlwind, to render his anger in fury, and his rebuke with flames of fire" (Isaiah 66:15). Fire was also used to represent God's presence and judgment, as seen in the verse from Isaiah and with Moses. Remember the burning bush? What about when the Law was given to Moses? God came down on Mt Sinai in the sight of all Israel in the form of fire before Moses went up to the mountain top (Ex 19:18). Even King David described the voice of God as flames of fire (Psalm 29:7).

In Acts 2, the fire is noted as *separated* or *divided* suggesting "one great flame representing the Spirit, which separates into many tongues of flame with one resting on each individual."[39] Notice Luke is writing in metaphors with phrases such as "*like* a mighty rushing wind" and "tongues *as of* fire." In other words, these were not literal flames because Luke says they were *as of fire* and probably not literal fire, but looked very much like it (2:3). And, though the wind was *like* a powerful and moving wind, it was not wind but God's Spirit.

All of the Jews present should have been familiar with each of the Old Testament passages we have mentioned and the disciples should have made the connection. One of the great things about preparing this study is I have read several different books on Pentecost, some written by Jewish men who believe Jesus is the Messiah. Many of these men document Jewish traditions and teachings, one of which concerned the giving of the Law. One such tradition the rabbis teach is that when giving the Law, God gave it in all seventy languages of the nations. The teaching indicates that God offered the Law to all nations but only Israel was willing to accept it. I do not know of this teaching in the Old Testament, however, I do think it is interesting that Jewish rabbis would teach this since God has from the beginning intended for Israel to make His Word available to all nations.

At Pentecost, God did give the message of His Spirit and salvation in every language. Of course, the largest percentage of the people present were Jews, though many of them were from various nations (as noted in Acts 2) and so would return to their homes with God's message. The New Covenant was established through the death, burial and resurrection of His Son and would be written on the hearts of God's people, not stone tablets. The Jews believe the Law was originally given on the day of Pentecost more than 1400 years prior, a law that could not be followed in the flesh. With the first Pentecost after Christ's ascension, God gave His Spirit in order that His children might be able to walk in righteousness. The day of Pentecost was the beginning of the Church, certainly a day to celebrate. And if Jewish tradition is correct, the Feast of Weeks (the Old Testament name for Pentecost) also marks the first giving of the Law. How fitting, because that would mean that on the same day God birthed His chosen nation of Israel, He chose to birth His Church.

Pentecost was a feast celebrating the harvest and what a harvest God gave on that day in Acts.

Acts 2:41 *"So those who received [Peter's] word were baptized, and there were added that day about three thousand souls."*

Peter, filled with the Holy Spirit, preached the sermon of his life and at the end God gave a harvest beyond anything they could have expected. I am sure no one present had ever celebrated the Feast of Weeks in such a miraculous way. Wouldn't you love to be able to ask Peter what his thoughts were after that experience? Do you think he, James, and John talked to one another about how they could see all Jesus had taught over three years? I think Peter looked at them and said 'Now I get it.' My prayer is that each one of us *gets it* enough to live it and share it, so others can say the same.

We have looked at the first four feasts given in Leviticus 23 and have seen how each one pointed to the first coming of Christ. We know that the Passover spoke of Christ's crucifixion, the Feast of Unleavened Bread pointed to His death, the Feast of Firstfruits looked to His resurrection and the Feast of Weeks (Pentecost) was a celebration of the harvests of God and the gift of His Spirit. There are three more feasts to study and I hope you are looking forward to them. I know I am.

Next week our focus will be the Feast of Trumpets.

Week 4 - **Feast of Trumpets**

Day 1 - The Day of Blowing Trumpets

So we have looked at the first four feasts commanded in Leviticus 23, all occurring in the spring of the year and fulfilled in the first coming of Christ. This week we will look at the first of the three fall feasts, what our English bibles call the Feast of Trumpets. It may be more familiar to some of you by the name Rosh Hashanah. Rosh Hashanah means "head of the year" and falls on the first day of the Hebrew month Ethanium (or Tishri postexile), which is September/October on our calendar. The name Rosh Hashanah was not applied to this feast until after the time of Christ, around the second century A.D. (over 1500 years after its institution). Scripture, however, does not refer to this feast as Rosh Hashanah or the Feast of Trumpets.

According to God's instructions to Moses, trumpet is simply a characteristic of the day but not a name. This feast does not seem to have an official name. All the other feasts are given a name (the Passover, the Feast of Unleavened Bread) but this feast has no title. It is, however, given a distinct characteristic, the blowing of trumpets, which became the basis for its name.

I believe there may be a reference to a name given in the following verse.

Numbers 29:1 "On the first day of the seventh month you shall have a holy convocation. You shall not do any ordinary work. It is a day for you to blow the trumpets, . . ."

Well, it may be more noticeable in the original Hebrew. The phrase *blow the trumpets* in Hebrew is 'teruwah' (or <u>t@ruw</u>'ah) which has a number of meanings including clamor, clanger of trumpets, a sound, signal, shout or alarm. Taking the word *day*, or 'yom' in Hebrew, along with the phrase 'blow the trumpets' we have the name *Day of Blowing* trumpets. Our English bibles simply reference it as the Feast of Trumpets.

I think before we go any further we need to look at God's full instructions for this feast. Please read the two passages noted below and fill in the blanks following each one.

On the first day of the seventh month there was to be a day of _____ (23:24).

This memorial was to be proclaimed with the _____ of trumpets (23:24).

They were to do no _____ work and present a _____ to God (23:25).

This feast was to be only one day and, based on this passage, its instructions seem to be pretty simple compared to the first four feasts. The first day of the seventh month there was to be a sacred assembly (or a Sabbath) called together by trumpet blasts with a burnt offering made to the Lord. We have already seen that the name for this feast comes from the fact that the trumpet announced its occurrence. Later in this week's study we will look more closely at the way trumpets are used in Scripture, but not today. Today, we are going to focus on the instructions for the feast.

Read Numbers 29:1-6 and complete the following:

The burnt offering included one young bull, _____ ram, _____ one-year old male lambs.

With each animal was a _____ offering of fine flour mixed with oil (29:2-4).

Also included was one male goat as a _____ offering (29:5).

These were to be in addition to the _____ and _____ offerings of the new moon (or daily and monthly offerings 29:6).

Obviously, the *burnt offering* mentioned in Leviticus 23 was not just one offering. According to Numbers 29, there were ten animals offered up for this feast, along with several grain and drink offerings. These offerings were to be *in addition to*, not instead of, the daily and monthly offerings. In a previous week's study we briefly looked at the various offerings required of the Israelites but we did not look specifically at the daily or monthly offerings. And, before you get a little unnerved, we are not going to do so now, at least not in any detail. Let me just explain that the first of every month was a type of Sabbath, or holy day, called the New Moon when a number of sacrifices were offered up in worship. In Numbers 28, we are given the instructions for the daily and monthly offerings (which you could read, it only takes a minute). If my math is correct (and it is probably not, but you will still get the idea), on the first day of the seventh month, the priests were to offer for Israel a total of 3 bulls, 2 rams, 16 male year-old lambs, 22 grain offerings of different specifications, 22 drink offerings of different specifications and 2 goats for the daily, monthly and feast offerings.

Keep in mind the offerings were the *proper* way to approach God. Since He is holy, He was to be approached through offerings made by a priest, God's appointed representative. It is so important that we remember worship is not about us, it is all about Christ and we must approach worship with a selfless attitude. We also must come to worship as instructed in God's Word. It is all about Him, we don't need to be comfortable, like the music, have a specific pew, none of that is important. What is important is honoring God.

Scripture states the sacrifices were to be offered up as a *pleasing aroma* to the Lord (Numbers 28:2). It might be worth looking at the first mention in Scripture of an offering as a *pleasing aroma*.

Gen. 8:20-21 *"Then Noah built an altar to the Lord and took some of every clean animal and some of every clean bird and offered burnt offerings on the altar. And when the Lord smelled the pleasing aroma, the Lord said in his heart, 'I will never again curse the ground because of man, for the intention of man's heart is evil from his youth. Neither will I ever again strike down every living creature as I have done."*

The first thing Noah did when he stepped off the ark was to build an altar and offer up sacrifices to God. No doubt this was an offering of thankfulness for God's protection, provision and deliverance for Noah and those with him on the ark. Offerings and sacrifices were a provision for worship and fellowship with God. It was the way God established for His people to approach Him. There are right and wrong ways to approach God. The Hebrew word for *pleasing* is 'nikhoakh' and suggests a soothing, settling or calming fragrance. Noah's offering calmed and maybe even changed God's anger directed at human sin.

But changed how? In Genesis 8, God's attitude changed from one bringing judgment that destroyed all life on the earth (except those on the ark) to promising never to destroy the earth by flood again. So with this *pleasing offering* we see the establishment of God's covenant and blessing on mankind. I do not know that Noah's offering actually changed God's mind about man because the passage states *the intention of man's heart is evil from his youth* (8:21). This tells us that mankind was not really any different after the flood (cf Gen 6:5). God's plan has always been to provide salvation or atonement for the world. He simply decided after the flood that a worldwide flood would not be the means of judgment again.

Though the *intention of man's heart* had not changed, God did find Noah's offering to be pleasing. The New Testament also speaks of a *pleasing* or acceptable offering. The sacrifice of Christ is described as *a fragrant offering and sacrifice to God* (Ephesians 5:2). Paul writes that Christians should "present your *bodies* as a living sacrifices, holy and *acceptable* to God, which is your spiritual worship" (Romans 12:1, emphasis added). In the Greek, the word *bodies* suggests the whole person, or body and soul. And it is a *living* sacrifice, as opposed to the Old Testament sacrifices which were slaughtered at the altar. We are alive in Christ who fulfilled the sin sacrifices of old, so there is no longer a need for blood to be shed. Christ's blood was sufficient once for all and therefore we should strive to honor God with our lives.

Our goal each day should be to live in such a way as to provide a pleasing aroma to God and not a stench. Sounds a bit abrupt I suppose, but think about it. Sin is obviously not pleasing to a holy God, quite the opposite. And the opposite of a pleasing aroma (or good smell) is one that stinks. We want to offer our lives, the way we live out each day, as *pleasing* to God. We are not able to do this in and of ourselves personally, but because of our Savior, the Lamb who was offered for us and who daily sits by the Father and intercedes for us. Yes, His job as the sacrifice for our sins was finished on the cross but He did not stop there. He now is our High Priest who loves us and continually speaks up as our defense before God. By His Spirit, we want to live our lives with a changed heart. What is the intention of your heart? Maybe you want to take a little time to reflect on that. Did the Lord delight in the way you lived out yesterday? It really is a question I believe is important enough to ask ourselves every morning.

Day 2 - The Trumpet signals Alarm

Israel's fifth annual feast consisted of a holy convocation, a day of solemn rest, the sounding of trumpets and an offering by fire. We saw yesterday that this was one day observed on the first day of the seventh month.

This feast takes place in what the Jewish people considered to be the most sacred month of the year. In the seventh month, Israel observed three of the seven annual feasts: the Feast of Trumpets, the Day of Atonement and the Feast of Tabernacles. It was in the seventh month that the high priest entered into the Holy of Holies, the most holy place, and made atonement for the people. This certainly would be reason to consider the seventh month to be a holy month.

Some believe the fact that it was the *seventh* month was also significant to it being a sacred month. There are differing opinions concerning the significance of numbers and not simply in the Bible. The early Egyptians believed in the symbolism of numbers. Seven is said to be the number of perfection, satisfaction, and rest. Though I am not encouraging any thought about numbers one way or another, I do think that most people would agree there is a frequency to the use of some numbers in Scripture, the number seven being one. For instance, the Lord rested on the *seventh* day of the creation week and later commanded it as a day of rest (Exodus 20:8-10). The Israelites were commanded to give the land a Sabbath every *seventh* year (Lev 25:4). The book of Revelation is full of sevens such as *seven* churches, seals, trumpets, and woes. The lampstand in the tabernacle had *seven* lamps. And, in Leviticus 23, God instituted *seven* annual feasts. There are other examples, but I think you get the point. So it is in the seventh month, Israel's holiest month, where we will focus our attention the next three weeks.

Along with not being given an official name, the first of the fall feasts also does not seem to have been given a specific reason for its observance. Remember that the spring feasts were observed as memorials of God's deliverance of the people from Egypt. Many believe a reason was not stated for this feast because it is obvious—it was a day to repent and prepare for the Day of Atonement (which follows ten days later). That would be one reason for the blowing of the trumpet, to alert (or alarm) the people the Day of Atonement was at hand. And that may be since trumpets were used by Israel for many various reasons and one was to sound an alarm.

Today, we are going to focus on trumpets and their different types and uses in Scripture. So, let's first go back to the nation of Israel's beginning, after her deliverance from Egypt, when God instructed Moses to make two silver trumpets.

Read Numbers 10:1-10 write all you learn about the silver trumpets.

_____

_____

_____

_____

In Israel's second year after leaving Egypt, God commanded the making of two silver trumpets that were to be used to coordinate the people's movement in the wilderness. According to Josephus, a Jewish historian, these silver trumpets were about twelve inches in length with a flared end. There were at least two ways of blowing these trumpets: simple and as an alarm. From this passage there was obviously a difference because God told them to blow with a _long blast not an alarm_ (10:7). The difference in the two may have been the difference in long notes verses short staccato blasts.

Keep in mind when the Israelites fled Egypt there were six hundred thousand men plus women and children (Exodus 12:37). It is possible the people totaled as many as two million. With this many people there had to be some orderly means of moving the people through the wilderness or they would be nothing more than an unruly mob. With God there is always order, so He gave Moses the means of directing the people and of signaling a message to His people.

These two silver trumpets were used for:

- summoning the people
- breaking camp
- gathering the people at the tent of meeting (when both were blown)
- summoning the heads of the twelve tribes (when one was blown)
- alerting the east side to set out (with the first alarm)
- alerting the south side to set out (with the second alarm)
- summoning an assembly (blowing a long blast, not an alarm)
- before going to war
- at the appointed feasts
- on the first of each month
- over the burnt offerings
- over the sacrifices of the peace offerings

Wow! Think about it. Moses was in the middle of the wilderness with possibly two million people headed to a land he had never seen, nor did he know its location and he needed to keep control. I wonder if he had given any thought to how he was going to ramrod all of those people through the wilderness. It really doesn't matter how Moses thought about handling it because obviously God knew the best way to direct the people—with trumpets.

And did you notice that God was more specific than just simply *when* to use the trumpets? He also told them *who* was to use them.

In the book of Numbers, Moses writes that it was the responsibility of the priests to blow the trumpets (Numbers 10:8). Blowing the trumpets at the time of the feasts or calling the people to assemble at the tent of meeting seems a natural responsibility for the priests since they would be overseeing these events. But the priests were to blow the trumpet even in war when going to battle. Now that seems so out of the ordinary for the priest's role. In our military today, a bugle is blown as a wakeup call or for retreat in the evening, but the soldier responsible for this is not a priest or chaplain. We would not think to put a priest, or minister, in such a position, yet God did, but why?

God told Moses that when Israel went to war, even in the Promised Land, they were to sound the trumpet alarm "that you may be remembered before the Lord your God, and you shall be saved from your enemies" (Numbers 10:9). The fact that priests were to be present for combat and God promised to save Israel from her enemies when the trumpets were blown tells us their battles were the Lord's or holy war. In other words, Israel's battles would be the Lord's and He would assure His people victory.[40]

Throughout the Old Testament, priests were instructed by God to be part of more than sacrifices and offerings. Joshua led the people to march around the walls of Jericho for six days. God told him "Seven priests shall bear seven trumpets of rams' horns before the ark. On the seventh day you shall march around the city seven times, and *the priests shall blow the trumpets*. And when they make a long blast with the ram's horn, when you hear the sound of the trumpet, then all the people shall shout with a great shout, and the wall of the city will fall down flat, and the people shall go up, everyone straight before him" (Joshua 6:4-5, emphasis added). It was not mighty warriors who blew the trumpets before the wall fell and the people took the city, it was seven priests. Not only were the priests present but also the ark of the covenant was with them as they marched and took the city. The ark symbolized God's presence and that the victory in battle was His doing. The conquest for the land was a holy war and, therefore, God's representatives to His people were to participate. The priests in battle suggest that none of us are excluded from fighting God's battles.

In reading Numbers 10, you probably noticed the silver trumpets were not the ones used at the wall of Jericho. These seven trumpets were the same type believed to have been used at the Feast of Trumpets and were made of a ram's horn. The passages in Leviticus 23 and Numbers 29 concerning this feast do not specifically name the ram's horn as the type of trumpet to be used, but Jewish tradition says it was the *shofar* (ram's horn). It may be that these passages do not specify the type of trumpet to be used because it is not what was important. What was important, I believe, was not the instrument as much as the *sound* of the trumpet. It was the sound of *one* trumpet that called the tribal chiefs together and the sound of *two* which summoned *all* the people to the tent of meeting. Yet, an assembly was to be summoned with a *long* blast not a *short alarm* sound. I believe that it was the *sound* of the trumpet that was the real issue.

And the reason I believe this is found in Exodus 19. You might remember we looked at the first verse of this passage last week.

_____

_____

_____

First, I want to address what I believe is a key point in this passage. In the first verse we are told the people have come into the wilderness of Sinai. Do you remember the story of Moses at the burning bush? Moses' first encounter with the Lord was on Mount Horeb, called the *mountain of God,* which is also known as Mount Sinai (Exodus 3:1). On this mountain God made a promise to Moses that He would bring the people out of Egypt and to that very mountain to serve Him (Exodus 3:12). In Exodus 19, we see the faithfulness of God to keep His promises to His people. Bringing Israel to that mountain was a sign that God had sent Moses there and that He would be with them (Exodus 3:12).

God brings Israel to the foot of the mountain seven weeks after their deliverance from Egypt, which we noted last week coincides with the Feast of Weeks. He brought them there to present His covenant and promise that they will be His treasured possession, a kingdom of priests, and a holy nation (Exodus 19:5-6). After meeting with God, Moses presents His words to the people, to which they agree to everything. The passage states that Moses consecrated the people so they would be ready to meet with God. The word *consecrate* in Hebrew is Qadash which means to be or make clean (ceremonially or morally)[41]. For two days, according to verse ten, the people were made ceremonially clean in order to be able to come before Holy God. And when the third day came, so did the fireworks.

Remember, it was a *long trumpet blast* that was to be used to summon the congregation together, which is exactly what is happening in this passage. Moses *brought the people out* to meet God, or summoned them. And the sound the people heard when Moses went up on the mountain was God speaking to Moses. It sounded like thunder, lightning, and *a trumpet blast* which grew louder and louder. So it seems to me that the sound of the trumpet may have been a reminder to the people of God's presence and His Word. Do you think that whenever they heard the trumpet summoning the congregation together there in the wilderness that they thought of God speaking to them?

Joshua Moss wrote concerning the Feast of Trumpets that "by Jewish tradition a person who has not listened to the shofar has not observed the day (or feast). Rabbis have said that the mitzvah (commandment) is not fulfilled by merely hearing the shofar, as if by accident, but that the hearer must listen with the specific kavanah (intention) of fulfilling the biblical commandment."[42] This feast day was to be a day of summoning the people to turn their minds and hearts back to God's Word. And it was to be a personal and intentional observance, one where the individual was *listening* for the sound of the trumpet. In the same way, we should be listening for the sound of God's Word with an *intention* of a personal relationship with Him and living as His Word instructs us to live. We have something the Old Testament Jews did not and that is God's Word documented for us in a single book. To know His Word, we must choose to study it, or be intentional about it. Just as the Jews believed each individual must listen for the sound of the trumpet on the feast day to know for certain they heard it, we need to look to the Word for ourselves, to be certain we hear it correctly. On the first day of the seventh month, the people of Israel expected to hear the trumpet. As God's people, we need to go to His Word and believe what He teaches from it.

We have only skimmed the surface concerning trumpets and the Day of Blowing. Tomorrow we will look further at trumpets.

Day 3 - The Shofar

I want to continue where we left off yesterday talking about trumpets, or specifically the trumpet used for this feast. Now trumpets were blown on the first of every month at the Temple for the new moon. The Psalmist wrote that Israel was to "Blow the trumpet at the new moon, at the full moon, on our feast day" (Psalm 81:3). I noted yesterday that the instructions for the Feast of Trumpets did not specifically identify the shofar as the trumpet to be blown but Jewish tradition was to use the ram's horn. It is possible that the above verse in Psalm 81 may have something to do with the use of the shofar. The Hebrew word for trumpet in this verse is *shofar* (or shophar). The reference *our feast day* is believed to be speaking of the Feast of Tabernacles, often referenced as '*the* feast,' which takes place on the 15th of the seventh month, just fifteen days after the Feast of Trumpets.

So if the feast mentioned in this verse is the Feast of Tabernacles, what does it have to do with the Feast of Trumpets? The New Moon was the first of every month, so the Feast of Trumpets fell on the New Moon of the seventh month. It seems very logical that if God required the shofar be used for the new moon and the Feast of Trumpets occurred on the new moon, the same horn would be used for both. It is also possible that the above verse was addressing the Feasts of Trumpets and the Feast of Tabernacles because it talks of the new and full moon. The full moon occurred in the middle of the month, around the 15th, and the Feast of Tabernacles was commanded to be held in the seventh month on the 15th day (or middle of the month).

There is only one record in Scripture of an actual observance of the Feast of Trumpets. Now this does not mean they only observed this feast one time, it is simply the only time we have a record of the details of its observance. In Ezra 3 the rebuilding of the Temple altar is recorded and the sacrifices are resumed by those Jews returning from the exile.

Read Ezra 3:1-6 and note any offerings or feasts re-instituted by Israel:

_____

_____

_____

This passage specifically names the Feast of Booths (or Tabernacles) as being observed by the people at that time. Though it does not name the *day of blowing trumpets*, it does state that it was the seventh month and that they kept the burnt offerings, regular offerings, the offerings at the new moon and *all the appointed feasts of the Lord* (3:5) which would include the Feast of Trumpets. Some of the people had returned from the exile to rebuild Jerusalem, though many remained in foreign lands. Even before the Temple rebuilding began, the altar was rebuilt and all the commanded offerings were observed because it had not been possible for at least seventy years while the people were in captivity. I wonder if their leaders, Zerubbabel and Jeshua, remembered how Israel had been originally delivered from slavery to travel to that land. And they also may have remembered how God had given instructions to Moses of all the offerings and feasts to be kept in the land. So upon their return, they did not waste any time repairing the altar. The repair was the priority of the people, because worshiping their God was most important to them. They observed all the holy days they had missed out on over their seventy years of captivity.

The altar was a priority in the nation's early years also.

> **Read Deuteronomy 27:4-8. What did Moses instruct the people to do when they entered the Promised Land?**

_____

_____

_____

When Moses spoke to the people before His death and their entering the land, he told them their first act when in the land was to build an altar to the Lord. Their priority upon stepping on that land was to worship the one who made it all possible for them to be there. Worship of God was the focus of Joshua's generation and it was no different for Zerubbabel's. The exiles from Babylon, now back in the land, knew what was important to their relationship with their God.

What an amazing sight that must have been to see all of the offerings and ordinances for the different feasts and sacrifices carried out by the people for the first time in so many years. I love the way the chapter begins with the people *gathered as one man* (Ezra 3:1). This is an expression of Israel's unity upon returning from their exile. They came together to worship their God as one man, united in observing all the ordinances having the same purpose, to worship their God.

This must have been a very long day observing all of the ordinances of the commanded offerings and feasts but I am sure the people did not think so. Traditionally, the synagogue services for the Feast of Trumpets (Rosh Hashanah) are some of the longest services. These services are known to continue for five hours or more. Like most feasts, the service consists of prayers and readings. There is an emphasis on God's majesty (kingship) and His remembrance of His everlasting covenant. One of the benedictions "focuses upon the key role of the shofar in the history of the nation. It speaks of Mt Sinai where the Lord first revealed Himself with the sound of the shofar."[43] It also speaks of "the end of days when God will again reveal Himself through fire and the sounding of the shofar as He sends the Messiah."[44] With this benediction is read a verse from Zechariah.

Zechariah 9:14 "Then the Lord will appear over them, and his arrow will go forth like lightning; the Lord God will sound the trumpet and will march forth in the whirlwinds of the south."

The prophet is speaking of how the Lord will return at the sound of the trumpet. The trumpet is associated with the presence of God, whether it be in giving His law to Moses or His second coming. Any time I hear a trumpet now, I will be reminded of my God, of His Word, and the hope I have of Jesus Christ's return.

Day 4 - The Last Trumpet

We ended yesterday with a verse from the Old Testament book of Zechariah, which is read with the benediction for this feast ceremony.

From Zechariah 9:14, list all the Lord will do.

_____

_____

_____

Earlier in this chapter, the prophet Zechariah speaks of the Messiah entering Jerusalem on a donkey, which is Jesus' triumphal entry into the city before His crucifixion or His first coming (Zechariah 9:9). And at the end of the chapter, the prophet speaks of when the Messiah will return at the sound of the trumpet or His second coming. The above verse (9:14) is speaking of the last occasion the Lord will blow the shofar, which is His final coming. Ancient Jewish tradition states that the resurrection of the dead will occur on Rosh Hashanah with the Lord's return.

Jesus taught of His second coming and the trumpet sounding.

In Matthew 24:30-31, what did Jesus say all the tribes of earth would see?

_____

_____

_____

And how will the Son of Man come?

_____

_____

_____

_____

_____

_____

_____

_____

_____

The apostle Paul also wrote about the last trumpet.

1 Corinthians 15:51-52 "Behold! I tell you a mystery. We shall not all sleep, but we shall all be changed, in a moment, in the twinkling of an eye, at the last trumpet. For the trumpet will sound, and the dead will be raised imperishable, and we shall be changed."

1 Thessalonians 4:16-17 "For the Lord Himself will descend from heaven with a cry of command, with the voice of an archangel, and with the sound of the trumpet of God. And the dead in Christ will rise first. Then we who are alive, who are left, will be caught up together with them in the clouds to meet the Lord in the air, and so we will always be with the Lord."

Amazing! From the Old Testament to the New Testament, the message of God is the same. This is what the apostle Paul believed and he had been raised with the best education afforded any Jewish man. But it was not his education that revealed this to him. He, with salvation and the Spirit of God, came to understand what God had said to His people.

The Lord's last trumpet will accomplish several things:
- It will gather an assembly to the Lord.
- It will sound God's battle alarm against Satan and a wicked world (Revelation 6:17).
- It will announce the coming of the Messiah.

The last trumpet of the Lord will be used in the same way prescribed by God in the Old Testament. In the wilderness the trumpets were used to gather God's people, sound a battle call and announce the Lord's appearance. On this feast day, the shofar served as a call to God's people to repent and to remember the holy day that was approaching, which was the Day of Atonement. This day would occur just nine days after the Feast of Trumpets, on the tenth of the same month. In my study I learned that for the Jewish people, Rosh Hashanah begins what they call the 'Days of Awe' when the people prayerfully repent before God. It also could speak of the final coming of the Lord, when a trumpet will sound, calling His true people to Him.

The Feast of Trumpets, or Rosh Hashanah, is a time to repent of sin, to remember to study God's Word and to live lives that will be pleasing to Christ. I know as New Testament Christians we are not required to observe this feast but we should live repentant lives that are pleasing to our God. This feast is only one day but its message should be lived out every day.

Next week we will look at the holiest day of Israel's year, the Day of Atonement. We could really spend weeks on this but we will condense it to just one week.

Week 5 - **The Day of Atonement**

Day 1 - The Day

Our sixth feast brings us to what is the most important of the Jewish Old Testament holy days. It may be better known to some as Yom Kippur, which means 'Day of Atonement.' The Jewish Talmud, which is a collection of rabbinic commentaries on the Jewish law, refers to the Day of Atonement as '*the* Day' because this was *the* day, the *only* day of the year that the high priest could enter the Holy of Holies. The instructions for this day are documented multiple times in the Old Testament. Today, we will look at two of these passages.

> **Please read Leviticus 23:26-32 and answer the following:**

The Day of Atonement took place on the _____ day of the _____ month (23:27).

Israel was to hold a _____ on this day and present a _____ offering (23:27).

The people were instructed to _____ themselves (23:27).

The people were to do no _____ on this day because it was the day when _____ was made for them before God (23:28).

Anyone who refused to deny himself (or not afflict himself) on this day was to be _____ from Israel (23:29).

The Lord promised to _____ anyone who did any work on this day (23:30).

_____

_____

_____

_____

The Day of Atonement occurs on the tenth of the seventh month of Israel's religious calendar. Last week we looked at the fact that the seventh month is considered holy to Israel and one reason is because the Day of Atonement occurs in this month. According to this passage, a food offering and an offering by fire were to be presented to the Lord. It was, like all Sabbaths, a day when the people would gather in a sacred assembly and when no work was allowed, with failure to comply bringing destruction from God.

God called this day the Day of Atonement. Atonement is the reconciliation of sinners to God by means of a blood sacrifice. Basically it is when the blood of an acceptable sacrifice made on this day brought _at-one-ment_ with God. But for the priest and people to participate in this day, they needed to acknowledge that they had sinned and their sin had caused separation from God. The sacrifice offered on this day was to make amends for those sins for one year.

There was one other command for this day in both passages which was to deny or afflict oneself. The phrase to _afflict yourselves, humble yourselves,_ or _afflict your souls,_ is actually a command to fast. It is really the only day in the year when Scripture _commands_ fasting, though it may be implied in other passages. It is possible, since specifics are not given, that food and liquids were not the only things from which the people were to abstain. It was not to be a day of pleasure but one in which sin was the focus so it is very probable that anything pleasurable was avoided. The Jewish people were to take this one day – a solemn Sabbath – to deny any pleasure and focus on the consequence of sin and on the repentance of sin. The consequence of sin was really two-fold: it separated the sinner from God and it required the life of a sacrifice.

In Numbers, we see that there was to be more than one offering presented on this day. On this day one bull, one ram and seven male lambs, all without defect, were offered as burnt offerings to the Lord. With each animal, a grain offering of various measurements of fine flour mixed with oil was presented along with one male goat as a sin offering. You may have noticed a pattern in the offerings for the holy days. For the feasts of Unleavened Bread, Weeks, Trumpets and Atonement, as well as the monthly offerings the same burnt and sin offerings were made with the exception of the bull, two were offered on all but Trumpets and Atonement, when only one was required. I do not know that it is explained why this order of sacrifices was required but the beginning chapters of Leviticus does give detail on the various offerings. There were different animals required based on if it was a sin offering and if the sin was intentional or not, committed by a leader, priest or common person, a peace offering or a praise offering. But I cannot say why this combination on feasts days. What I know is that one key message of the Bible is sacrificial atonement. The cost of atonement was the death of a sacrifice, that is why Paul wrote that _the wages of sin is death_ (Romans 6:23).

The Day of Atonement was a day when all of Israel was to consider sin. It was a day of serious contemplation of one's relationship with God. The seriousness of this day can be seen in the command given concerning work. The Lord told Moses "whoever does any work on that very day, that person *I will destroy* from among his people" (Lev 23:30, emphasis added). Anyone who ignored this command and chose to work would be destroyed by God. This was a day to be approached with absolute reverence and obedience. The seriousness of sin meant this day was one of fasting, not feasting. This was not a day for celebration or rejoicing, but one of affliction and sorrow over sin. It was the day when the high priest would enter by the blood of a bull and goat to the Holiest Place and receive forgiveness for himself first and then for the people.

King David may have had the Day of Atonement in mind when he penned these words:

"Blessed is the one whose transgression is forgiven, whose sin is covered. Blessed is the man against whom the Lord counts no iniquity, and in whose spirit there is no deceit." (Psalm 32:1-2).

These verses give an excellent description of what should be our response to having our sins forgiven—the realization that we are truly blessed or joy within our spirit. Joy because when God covers sin, He blots it out or completely removes it. That was the point of the Day of Atonement, that the sins of the people of Israel would be removed until the next year.

Day 2 - Entering the Holiest Place

This week's study is of the most holy day of the year for the nation of Israel. The people were required to participate in the day by fasting from personal pleasures and observing it as a solemn day of rest. All other feast days were days or weeks of celebration, but this was to be a day of sorrow. This was a day for the people to realize their sins, one of sorrow because they recognized they had sinned against God. On the Day of Atonement the nation of Israel would consider the sins, impurities and transgressions of an unholy people desiring mercy from a most holy God. That is why the command is given for the people to afflict themselves, which is to deny themselves pleasure.

The Day of Atonement was the day when the sins of Israel would be covered for the year. In the Old Testament, the most commonly used Hebrew word for *atonement* is from the root word 'kaphar', which means *to cover* or *make reconciliation*.[45] The covering of sin meant that the penalty no longer had to be paid by the offender because a substitute was given in his/her place. In the Old Testament the substitute was an animal, such as a lamb, bull, or goat.

Yesterday, you looked at two short passages of Scripture that addressed the Day of Atonement. The Lord's detailed instructions for this day are documented for us in Leviticus sixteen. Let's begin today by reading through Leviticus 16 (a couple of times would be wise). While the emphasis in yesterday's passages was more on the principal sacrifices and fasting, today's passage gives the detailed instructions for the purification for sins that only the high priest could administer as God's representative.

In order to enter the sanctuary, the high priest had to bring a young _____ for a _____ offering and a _____ for a burnt offering (16:3).

The first thing the high priest did before entering the tabernacle was to _____ himself and then put on the _____ garments (16:4).

The garments included the linen _____, linen undergarments, the linen _____ and a linen _____ (16:4).

He was to take two male goats for Israel's _____ offering and one ram for a _____ offering (16:5).

The high priest was to offer a _____ for his personal sin offering (16:6).

The instructions for the Day of Atonement in Leviticus 16 begin with a reference to the death of Aaron's oldest sons Nadab and Abihu, who were struck dead by God because they had *offered unauthorized fire before the Lord* (see Lev 10). After the author mentions the death of Aaron's eldest sons, he documents God's warning to Aaron that he should never enter the Holy of Holies behind the veil any time he wanted, but only at the time and in the way the Lord commanded. Aaron's sons tried to worship God in a way that He did not accept and the result was their death. The positioning of these two statements, the sons' deaths and the high priest's warning, suggest that Aaron's sons may have attempted to go behind the veil with the unholy fire. We do not know this for sure but certainly their deaths would have been a vivid example to Aaron and any high priests who followed him not to take the Lord's instructions lightly, but to follow them exactly. We are not to worship any way we want or that is easy for us. No, we must approach God in worship only in ways He has deemed acceptable. If nothing else, the story of Nadab and Abihu shows this is a most serious matter. After the warning, instructions were given for the correct way for the high priest to enter the holiest place.

The high priest, as the people's representative, had access into the presence of God because the Lord had invited him. No ordinary priest could enter, only the high priest and only on this specific day of the year. On the Day of Atonement, the first thing the high priest would do was bathe himself and put on appropriate clothing. He could not stand before God in his own personal garments or garments of his choosing but had to wear clothing specified by God. Charles Spurgeon wrote that these clothes were of no expense to the priest and required no skill from him, he just simply put them on so it was not something of which he could boast, quite the contrary, it should have been very humbling. On this day he was *not* to put on the beautifully adorned garments with the breastplate, ephod, or coat of checker work (Exodus 28:4). The breastplate and ephod were made of gold, blue, purple and scarlet yarn and all of these were *for glory and for beauty* (Exodus 28:2). Instead, the high priest would wear only the linen coat, linen undergarment, linen sash and the linen turban, all very plain clothing. The high priest was not to enter the presence of the Most Holy God with glory and beauty, but simply with humility. He was presenting the offerings for the forgiveness of sins, which was no reason to be proud. Again how we approach God is so important, not with pride but humility.

We cannot serve God in our own righteousness because it is *like a polluted garment* before Him (Isaiah 64:6). The high priest was to put on garments provided for him and, like him, we put on righteousness that is provided for us by Jesus Christ. But I also want you to see that the physical cleansing of the priest was a picture of his desire for spiritual cleansing from God. And it was a foreshadowing of Christ as was the entire Day of Atonement.

> **What does Hebrews 10:19-22 tell us about drawing near to God?**

_____

_____

_____

Just as the priest would have to be physically cleansed before entering into God's presence, we also need cleansing, spiritual cleansing. This comes once our hearts are sprinkled clean from guilt and our bodies washed with pure water that is only available because of the blood of our high priest, Jesus Christ and His love offering on the cross. Faith that is trusting in what Christ did on the cross was enough that we might be *at-one* with God the Father. I hope you are seeing how the entire Bible is one story pointing to and climaxing in Jesus Christ. The Day of Atonement is one part of that story in which every element of it is a foreshadowing of the Son.

> **Read Leviticus 16:11-14 describing the personal offering of the high priest in the Holiest Place.**

After the physical cleansing and putting on of the humble garments, the high priest would slaughter a bull as a sin offering for himself and his household because he was guilty of sin just like the people and could not enter behind the veil without first dealing with his sins. The veil separated the outer area of the Tabernacle, known as the Holy Place, where the priests would enter daily to attend to the lampstand, table of showbread, and incense altar. This veil was a very thick curtain put in place to make certain no one came near or even looked upon the Most Holy Place.

The high priest would take coals from the brazen altar in the outer courtyard in a censor along with two handfuls of incense and go into the Holy of Holies. The brazen altar was where the sacrifices were offered and its fire had been set by God from heaven, making it *holy fire*. Upon entering behind the veil, he would put the incense in the censor causing a cloud or fog to cover the mercy seat over the ark. The passage states that he was to do this so that he *would not die* (Lev 16:13). The fog from the incense would keep the high priest from clearly seeing God's presence over the mercy seat.

_____

_____

_____

God promised that He would meet with them above the mercy seat between the two cherubim, which were positioned on each end of the ark facing one another. This was the place where Israel, represented by the high priest, could meet with God. It was made of pure gold and was the physical representation of God's presence. The mercy seat was also known as the atonement cover. Both _mercy_ seat and _atonement_ cover were very appropriate terms as atonement is _to be covered over_ and that covering for us comes by means of God's mercy.

Entering the Holy of Holies any other way than that dictated by God would cause the high priest's death. In order to be sure that the high priest was alive while behind the veil, God told Moses to put bells on the hem of the high priest's garment so he could be heard moving about and those outside would know that he was alive (Exodus 28:33-35). I wonder if He did this because He wanted to emphasize the seriousness of entering correctly or because He knew some would enter sinfully and be struck down. Or maybe it was both. Jewish tradition states that a rope would be tied around the leg of the high priest before he entered the Holiest Place so that if he were struck dead, they could retrieve his body without going in and causing their own death.

What was the high priest to do once the cloud covered the mercy seat? (Lev 16:14)

_____

_____

_____

How many times was he to do this? _____

Once the incense cloud had covered the mercy seat, the high priest would take blood from the sacrificed bull and sprinkle it on the front of the mercy seat with his finger seven times. Remember last week we saw the number seven is the number of perfection. The blood was sprinkled seven times to _atone_ for the high priest's own sins and the sins of his household _before_ he could act on behalf of the people. From this we see that even the one thought to be the holiest among us is just a sinner.

Hebrews 5:1-4 "For every high priest chosen from among men is appointed to act on behalf of men in relation to God, to offer gifts and sacrifices for sins. He can deal gently with the ignorant and wayward, since he himself is beset with weakness. Because of this he is obligated to offer sacrifice for his own sins just as he does for those of the *people. And no one takes this honor for himself, but only when called by God, just as Aaron was."*

The writer of Hebrews makes it clear the high priest was a man with weaknesses just like every other man. Since he was a sinner himself, he would understand the waywardness of others. His was a position that was appointed by God, not men and not because of anything he had done, so he should not be proud or boast. The high priest was a picture of Jesus, who is our high priest, but Jesus' priesthood is a more powerful, a more perfect, and a more permanent priesthood than that of Aaron. Jesus is a high priest without sin. And the priesthood of Jesus Christ is an eternal priesthood, lasting forever. I want to take a moment and look at Jesus as our high priest.

Look up the following verses and note anything you learn about the priesthood of Jesus Christ.

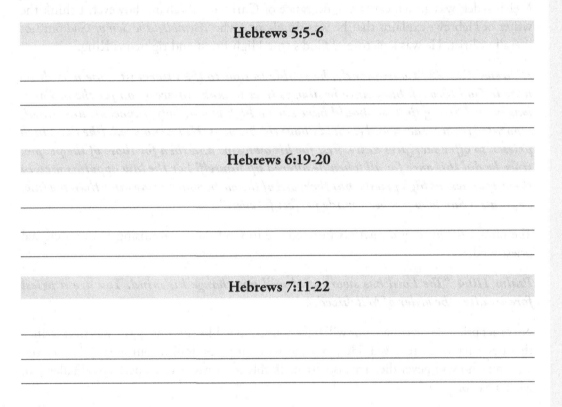

Hebrews 5:5-6

_____

_____

_____

Hebrews 6:19-20

_____

_____

_____

Hebrews 7:11-22

_____

_____

_____

Jesus did not exalt himself to the priesthood but was appointed by God, just as Aaron was appointed by God. But Jesus' priesthood is eternal after the order of Melchizedek. Jesus was not of the tribe of Levi as the high priest was commanded to be, but of the tribe of Judah, the kingly tribe. The writer of Hebrews explains that the appointment of the high priest followed the law but the law "made nothing perfect" (Heb 7:19). Through Jesus, there is a better hope because His priesthood is perfect and permanent.

But who was Melchizedek? He was the king of Salem and priest of the Most High God to whom Abraham gave a tithe of his spoils (Genesis 14). His name means *king of righteousness* and the name of his city, Salem, means *peace*, therefore, he was the king of righteousness and peace. According to the writer of Hebrews, he *resembled the Son of God*, which would indicate that he was a type or Old Testament picture of Christ.

Hebrews 7:3 "He (Melchizedek) is without father or mother or genealogy, having neither beginning of days nor end of life, but resembling the Son of God he continues a priest forever."

The Old Testament does not give an account of Melchizedek's genealogy or of his priesthood's beginning or ending, so his priesthood *appears* to continue forever (Heb 7:3b). The Levitical priests of Israel were temporary, each one replaced upon his death by the next in line. In contrast, Christ's priesthood *is* eternal, a permanent priesthood, for He will never be replaced ("but he holds his priesthood permanently, because he continues forever" Heb 7:24). Because there was no evil or corruption in him, his was a perfect priesthood; therefore, he never needed to enter the Holiest Place on his own behalf. Some believe Melchizedek was a preincarnate appearance of Christ to Abraham; however, I think the writer of Hebrews explains that he was simply one who *resembled the Son of God* but not literally Christ. He was a picture of God's true High Priest and righteous King.

Hebrews 7:25-28 "Consequently, he is able to save to the uttermost those who draw near to God through him, since he always lives to make intercession for them. For it was indeed fitting that we should have such a high priest, holy, innocent, unstained, separated from sinners, and exalted above the heavens. He has no need, like those high priests, to offer sacrifices daily, first for his own sins and then for those of the people, since he did this once for all when he offered up himself. For the law appoints men in their weakness as high priests, but the word of the oath, which came later than the law, appoints a Son who has been made perfect forever."

The phrase *the word of the oath* is in reference to God's oath promising Him an eternal priesthood.

Psalm 110:4 "The Lord has sworn and will not change his mind, You are a priest forever after the order of Melchizedek."

No other priest has ever had, nor will have, a testimony like this one. Jesus was the sacrifice that never has to be renewed. He is a priest without peers. Jesus is our great priest as well as King who will never die. This is why he is able to minister to us perfectly. Hallelujah, what a Savior!

Though I would rather keep going we will stop here and continue with the sacrifices offered for the people tomorrow. Maybe you might want to take a few moments to reflect on the mercy of God and the preciousness of salvation.

Day 3 - The Lord's Goat

Yesterday, we saw that a bull was to be offered for the sins of the high priest and his household. Did you notice that in Leviticus 16 Moses repeats seven times that the priest was to bring an offering for himself? Well, he does, twice in verse six, three times in verse 11, and once in verses seventeen and twenty-four. It appears he was stressing the point that Aaron needed to atone for his own sins like every other man. Sometimes we have the tendency to put men in certain positions on pedestals, regardless of the facts about the person. I believe we are to support our pastoral staffs and by that I mean financially, prayerfully, and any other way. But I also think we need to be careful and remember pastors are men and need accountability like every other human. We also need to watch our expectations of these men. They are God's servants, not God. They cannot and should not be expected to be all things to all people within their congregations. If we do, we set them up to fail and that is in no way support. This passage seems to stress the point that the high priest, though he held a position of honor, was simply a sinful man.

Once the high priest slaughtered the bull, he took the bull's blood behind the veil of the Tabernacle and sprinkled it on the mercy seat seven times for himself and his family's cleansing then he could offer the people's sacrifice. After the high priest had offered the bull for his sins and his families' sins, he made the offering for the people's sins.

Read Leviticus 16:7-10, 15-19 and answer the following:

What was the high priest to bring for the people's sins (16:7)?

_____

_____

_____

Why was he to cast lots (16:8-10)?

_____

_____

_____

The high priest would take two male goats and place them at the entrance of the tabernacle. He then cast lots to determine which of the goats was *for the Lord* and which goat was *for Azazel*. It was believed that casting lots meant the Lord made the decision, or the lot would fall the way the Lord wanted.

Now don't go scanning through the index of your bible looking for a previous reference to Azazel because I am pretty sure you won't find one. The meaning of the word (Azazel) is believed to be a combining of the words meaning "goat" and "going away" or "goat that goes away."[46] Some translations refer to this as the *scapegoat*. We will spend the remainder of today looking at the *Lord's goat*, leaving the scapegoat for tomorrow.

The lot that fell to the Lord's goat meant death for that animal. This was the goat which would be sacrificed on the brazen altar for the sins of the people. Once it was slaughtered, the goat's blood was taken into the Holy of Holies and the priest would do with it as he had done with the blood of the bull, he would sprinkle the goat's blood *on the atonement cover* or mercy seat (Lev 16:15).

After the sins of the people had been atoned for, the priest would cleanse the items within the tabernacle (the table for showbread, the lampstand, the incense altar) with the blood of the bull and goat, then the Tabernacle itself because of the *uncleanness and rebellion of the Israelites* (16:16). This is a reference to the true meaning of sin, which is anything contrary to the will of God. By not living within the commandments of the Lord, the people were rebelling against His covenant. The Tabernacle had to be cleansed because it dwelt among an unholy people and was serviced by an unholy priesthood.

So on this day, the high priest went in to the holiest place and offered atonement for himself, for the people, and cleansing for the place that was serviced by unholy men. Just as blood was sprinkled on the mercy seat, it was also sprinkled on the objects inside the tent. No one but Aaron (or the high priest) could be inside the tabernacle during this time because there was only one mediator between God and the people. This mediator was the man of God's choosing, the high priest. But the people were not idle while he was inside. They would be outside in the Tabernacle courtyard worshiping God, praying, lamenting over their sins, and awaiting the exit of their high priest.

Once the priest had finished inside the Tabernacle, he had more to do in the courtyard.

What item would he make atonement for in the courtyard (16:18-19)?

_____

_____

_____

Why would he do this (16:19)?

_____

_____

_____

Once finished inside the Tabernacle, he would continue by cleansing the brazen altar. He did this by taking the blood of the bull and goat and putting it on the horns of the altar. Again, this was done because of the uncleanness of the people.

The Day of Atonement was a very bloody day providing the people a disturbing visual of sin's cost. But the fact is that death and suffering are the result of sin. The sight and smell of that day must have been awful. Most of us are horrified at the sight or thought of blood because it makes us think of pain or death. We should be as appalled at the thought of sin as we are at the thought of bloodshed. On this day, the blood was to be shocking and horrifying to the people, making them think about the horror and destruction of sin. Blood represents life and it's shedding represented death. So God assigned the shedding of blood for the means of atonement.

Leviticus 17:11 "For the life of the flesh is in the blood, and I have given it for you on the altar to make atonement for your souls, for it is the blood that makes atonement by the life."

Hebrews 9:22 "Indeed, under the law almost everything is purified with blood, and without the shedding of blood there is no forgiveness of sins."

The offering of sacrifices was a gift of God giving His people the means of atonement. That atonement could only be achieved through the shedding of blood. But, under the law, that sacrifice had to be made over and over again because no one sacrifice would satisfy the debt. With Christ, there was one perfect blood sacrifice made once for all because His sacrifice was sufficient to appease the penalty for all sin. For that, I am more grateful than I can say.

Day 4 - The Scapegoat

Yesterday, we looked at the offering of the first goat, otherwise known as the Lord's goat. Today, we will begin by looking at Azazel's goat. I noted previously that the word *Azazel* indicates the idea of escape. It became known as the scapegoat because, unlike the Lord's goat, this goat actually escaped death and was driven into the wilderness, carrying away the sins of Israel. But there is controversy over the meaning of the name Azazel. Jewish tradition says that Azazel was the name of a fallen angel. For this reason, some believe it is a reference to Satan. But my question is why would Satan *carry away* the sins of Israel? Most scholars believe the first definition is accurate, that the word carries the idea of escape and so we will reference this second goat as the scapegoat.

When the lot was cast and determined which goat was the Lord's and which was the scapegoat, tradition records that a crimson strip of wool was tied to one of the horns of the scapegoat. This was to be sure it was not sacrificed by mistake. Once the yarn was tied to its horn, the goat was then turned to face the people. I don't know why this was done but maybe they would be reminded of why there was a need for the scapegoat if they had to look at this innocent animal face-to-face.

Once the Lord's goat was sacrificed, all attention was placed on the scapegoat.

What was done with the scapegoat (Lev. 16:20-22)?

_____

_____

_____

The high priest would lay his hands on the head of the scapegoat and confess Israel's wickedness and sin over it. Several passages in Leviticus dealing with sacrifices speak of the offerer laying a hand on the sacrificial animal, which symbolized the transfer of sin onto the sacrifice. In every passage I read, it is hand (singular) except the passage on the Day of Atonement where the word is plural. Also, on the Day of Atonement it was not the individual offerer who laid his hand on the animal. On this day the high priest represented all of the people.

After the sins of the nation were verbalized over the scapegoat, the goat would be led into the wilderness symbolically carrying away Israel's sin. Josephus describes the scapegoat as the expiation for the sins of the entire nation.[47] Expiation means to make amends or satisfy wrongs, which is what is at the heart of this day. The Lord's goat was a picture of the *means* for atonement which was by the blood of a sacrifice, and the scapegoat pictured the *effect* of atonement or the removal of sin. Both of these find their fulfillment in Christ's sacrifice on the cross.

David's writings express the meaning and result of the scapegoat.

Psalm 103:11-12 *"For as high as the heavens are above the earth, so great is his steadfast love toward those who fear him; as far as the east is from the west, so far does he remove our transgressions from us."*

According to Charles Spurgeon, the Day of Atonement happened once a year, not daily or monthly, because it was a picture that Jesus should die once for our sins. Every morning and evening of every day sacrifices were offered as a reminder to the people of their need for a sacrifice, but the Day of Atonement was a picture of the once-for-all sacrifice of the Messiah. It was also an offering made on an *appointed* day, not to be made randomly at anyone's leisure or convenience.

In the same way, Christ's Day of Atonement for our sins was predestined by God before creation. Just as the high priest came humbly before God, so Jesus came, not with the glory of heaven but stripped of even his common man's robe. The scapegoat was sent out of the camp carrying the symbolic sins of Israel. Like the second goat, Jesus was sent outside the camp as he was crucified just outside of Jerusalem. The writer of Hebrews states "So Jesus also suffered *outside the gate* in order to sanctify the people through his own blood" (Hebrews 13:12, emphasis added). On the Day of Atonement, only the High Priest administered the sacrifices and blood of the atonement. Jesus alone was the atonement for the world's sin, no other sacrifice is worthy.

Try to picture this day from the high priest's viewpoint. Everywhere he looked, he saw blood. In the outer court, the brazen altar would be covered in blood from multiple animals' death and there would be bowls of blood at its base. Inside the Tabernacle, the incense altar just in front of the veil would have blood sprinkled on it. On the other side of the veil, there would be blood on the ark of the covenant. There would probably have been blood on the veil itself from the sprinkling on the mercy seat. Even the linen clothing of the priest would be spattered with blood, so when he came out of the Tabernacle the people would see the blood and the result of their sins. This was not a day for the faint-hearted. It was "God's intent to awaken in man a great disgust of sin, by making him see that it could only be put away by suffering and death."[48] The sight of Jesus on the cross would have been a bloody visual of sin's cost. But again sin could only be put away by suffering and death permanently by the one perfect sacrifice. And now there is no longer a need for a sacrifice because the perfect atonement was made covering all sin for all time.

But it wasn't just the high priest or even the people who saw the blood. The high priest could not enter the Holy of Holies, the place of God's presence, without blood. It was Jehovah seeing the blood of the bull and goat that meant atonement was made for Israel. And, at

Calvary, it was Christ's presentation of His blood before God which provided salvation. Access to God was by virtue of the blood of a sacrifice. Our access to God is by virtue of the blood of Christ, who is our atonement.

When the high priest was allowed to enter the Holy of Holies once a year, he presented the blood of a bull and a goat. Jesus entered with his own blood. On the day of His sacrifice, the veil was torn from top to bottom because access to God had been accomplished.

Hebrews 10:19-22 "Therefore, brothers, since we have confidence to enter the holy places by the blood of Jesus, by the new and living way that he opened for us through the curtain, that is, through his flesh, and since we have a great priest over the house of God, let us draw near with a true heart in full assurance of faith, with our hearts sprinkled clean from an evil conscience and our bodies washed with pure water."

Christ's priestly work accomplished what could not be done for thousands of years—access to God for all. Those who are His, saved by His blood and God's mercy, have received the privilege of following Christ into the holy place. We know from the writer of Hebrews that "it is impossible for the blood of bulls and goats to take away sin" (Heb 10:4). But Jesus "entered once for all into the holy places, not by means of the blood of goats and calves but by means of his own blood, thus securing an eternal redemption. For if the blood of goats and bulls, and the sprinkling of defiled persons with the ashes of a heifer, sanctify for the purification of the flesh, how much more will the blood of Christ, who through the eternal Spirit offered himself without blemish to God, purify our conscience from dead works to serve the living God" (Heb 9:12-14).

Christ lived a sinless life and died a sinner's death in order to *save his people from their sins* (Matt 1:21). Just like the Lord's goat on the Day of Atonement, Jesus paid the penalty we deserved to pay for our sin. And like the scapegoat on that same day, He took our sins away and overcame the separation between God and us caused by our sins.

Colossians 1:13-14 "He has delivered us from the domain of darkness and transferred us to the kingdom of his beloved Son, in whom we have redemption, the forgiveness of sins."

Everything about the Day of Atonement pointed to Jesus Christ. The blood of the bull, the Lord's goat, the scapegoat and even the high priest himself was a picture of Christ. Before the creation of the world, God determined how atonement would be brought to the world and who would ultimately provide our access to Him. It was Israel's most holy day of the year which pointed to the most Holy One. Aren't you glad you live on this side of the cross?

I wish we could continue with this day, there is so much more I have learned in my study. But you don't have to stop. Take time before you start next week's feast to read over Leviticus 16 again and do your own study on Hebrews 9 and 10. You will be blessed by it, I promise.

The Day of Atonement was the sixth of the seven feasts presented in Leviticus 23. Next week we look at the last of the annual feasts, the Feast of Tabernacles.

Week 6 - **The Feast of Tabernacles**

Day 1 - Sukkot

So we have come to the last feast we will look at in this study. There are feasts that were added to Israel's year, but our focus for this study has been only those explained in Leviticus 23. Many of you may be ready to celebrate that we are finished. Hopefully, this study has been helpful. I have enjoyed every minute of it.

The final feast given in Leviticus 23 is the Feast of Tabernacles, also known as the Feast of Booths or the Feast of Ingathering. This is also the third (and last) of the pilgrimage feasts requiring the Jewish men to attend in Jerusalem (see Deuteronomy 16—the others being the Feast of Unleavened Bread and the Feast of Weeks). This final of the seven feasts was joyous and community-oriented.

God established the Feast of Tabernacles "so that Israel, among other things, would be reminded annually of His provision of a harvest that supplied the food for the rest of the year."[49] We saw in week three of our study that the Feast of Weeks was associated with the wheat harvest, while this last feast included the remaining produce of Israel but could also include the latter wheat crop. Israel's land yielded a variety of crops including grapes, dates and figs. "The Lord's festivals reminded His people that one God created all things and rules over all things. The festivals remind God's people that He provides rain in its season and a harvest in its season . . ."[50] Yet, the harvest was not the only reason God established the Feast of Tabernacles. Our first passage will reveal another reason the feast was established.

Read Leviticus 23:33-43 and fill in the blanks below.

This feast took place on the _____ day of the _____ month (23:34).

It was to be a _____ _____ and, like all Sabbath days, the people were to do no _____ (23:35).

They were to present a food offering to the Lord for _____ days (23:36).

A second _____ was to be held on the eighth day (23:36).

It was a _____ assembly and no ordinary _____ was to be done (23:36).

The feast began once they had gathered the _____ of the land (23:39).

It was to be a _____ throughout the generations (23:41).

The people were to dwell in _____ for seven days (23:42). They did this to remember when God made the people dwell in booths in the _____(23:43).

On the 15th of Tishri (September/October), just five days after the Day of Atonement, Israel celebrated the seventh feast. Did you notice there was a major difference from the Day of Atonement? The Feast of Tabernacles was the last of the three feasts observed in the seventh month, with the first two focused on Israel's need for atonement. The Day of Atonement was a very solemn day, more along the line of a funeral than a celebration. This feast, however, was to be a joyous time for Israel to celebrate God's provision and the forgiveness of their sin debt. It was observed for eight days total, with no ordinary work to occur on the first and the eighth day. These two days were to be observed as Sabbaths. On the in-between days, offerings were made to the Lord in addition to the daily offerings.

This feast is known in Hebrew as *Sukkot*. The word *sukkot* is the plural of *sukkah*, meaning tabernacle or booth. It was a temporary shelter like the kind made by shepherds while out with their sheep feeding in various pastures. The shelters could be easily assembled or broken down as they moved about. The people would literally take up temporary residence for one week in fragile booths made from palms and leafy branches. Many of these were built on the flat roofs of their homes, for those who actually lived in Jerusalem. The roof of the booth was made of sticks and leaves allowing the stars to be visible, as well as a little rain to come through.

But why did they have to literally live in booths? This feast was a reminder to the people of Israel's deliverance from Egypt and its dependence on God as they wandered through the wilderness forty years living in booths, or temporary dwellings, that they would take up each time the cloud of God moved. This feast was a yearly reminder that God is the Great Shepherd who chose to *tabernacle among them*, provide for them, protect them and ultimately bless them, even in their wilderness time. During these seven days, they would move out of their homes, some even left their cities for Jerusalem, and they lived in small huts, where I am certain conversations would take place about the wilderness wanderings of their ancestors. They may have taught their children about God's miraculous provision of heavenly bread and quail that literally dropped outside their doors. It is conceivable that they would talk about water that was provided from a rock or that was purified with a tree trunk. And they would have remembered how God directed their ancestors with His cloud by day and fire by night (the perfect MapQuest).

The people were to live in booths for seven days, but not on the eighth day. On the eighth day it would seem that they were back in their houses. This would be a reminder of their coming into the Promised Land with all its benefits, one being that they would no longer be living in huts but able to settle down in homes. This would be a huge reason for celebration on the eighth day of the feast.

God knew that when the people settled in the Promised Land, they would become comfortable in their houses and forget about their need for Him. Moses warned the people before they entered the Promised Land not to forget their God.

Deuteronomy 6:10-13 "And when the Lord your God brings you into the land that He swore to your fathers, to Abraham, to Isaac, and to Jacob, to give you—with great and good cities that you did not build, and houses full of all good things that you did not fill, and cisterns that you did not dig, and vineyards and olive trees that you did not plant—and when you eat and are full, then take care lest you forget the Lord, who brought you out of the land of Egypt, out of the house of slavery. It is the Lord your God you shall fear. Him you shall serve and by His name you shall swear."

We become comfortable and tend to forget how we got that way. That is what Moses warned them of as he pointed out several times that their comfort would not be by anything they had done but all would be by the hand and mercy of God.

Read through the above passage from Deuteronomy and underline every phrase that Moses points out something the people benefited from that was not of their own doing.

I count four—they would live comfortably in cities they did not build, houses they did not furnish, wells they did not dig and vegetation they did not plant. God had brought them into *a land flowing with milk and honey* of His creation (Deuteronomy 6:3b). It is so easy for us to become complacent and forget about God. Oh, don't get me wrong, we remember to go to church or choir and we don't do anything *blatantly* wrong, at least not by our standards. But we don't remember Him and what He does for us every day. It is when life is easy or comfortable that we tend to rely on ourselves and forget our need for Christ. We need to be much more careful and cautious in the less difficult times that we not become self-confident and forget Christ is our treasure, our provider, our Savior and our rest.

I know it seems unlikely as we go through this study that we would not put Christ first, but we are human just like the Israelites. It happened to them over and over, it happens to us unless we focus on Christ daily. The Lord has brought me to a point where I realize that I relate to the Israelites far more than I ever thought. Please understand, I am not making excuses for their sins, but understand and try to compare myself to see where I am guilty of the same sins. That is one very important reason why we should study the Bible, because we need to learn from the history of others.

It is important for me (and you) to remember the things the Lord has done in my life and for me, how He has blessed me, the lessons He has taught me, the grace He has shown me, and how I am a different person in Him. God did not want His people to get lazy in their walk with Him and fall into sin so He gave them reminders throughout the year. Why? Because He loves His people and desires the best for them. He is the best thing for us, that is a day-to-day relationship with the one true God who desires to *dwell* in our midst and be part of our everyday lives.

Day 2 - A Joyful Celebration

We looked yesterday at how the Feast of Tabernacles reminded the people of Israel of God's provision during the wilderness wanderings when they lived in booth-like dwellings, hence the feast's name. It reminded them of His ongoing blessings. This was a feast that also celebrated the last agricultural season of each year when the people reaped from the vineyards, olive orchards and vegetable crops, all of which were provided by God.

There were a large number of offerings made during the week this feast was celebrated. Sacrifices were central to worship for ancient Israel and this feast was an example of just that. The same number of rams, lambs and goats were offered on each of the first seven days, but the number of bulls decreased by one each day until the eighth, when only one bull was sacrificed.

Read Numbers 29:12-40 for an explanation of the offerings on this week.

Based on the number of animal sacrifices offered during this feast, it seems obvious that this was an important week. I count a total of 71 bulls, 15 rams, 105 lambs, and 8 goats sacrificed over eight days, which does not include all the grain, drink, goodwill or daily offerings. According to Dennis Cole, the accompanying grain and oil added up to approximately twenty-two bushels of fine flour and sixty-five gallons of olive oil.[51] What a sight it must have been in Jerusalem that week with all the booths set up on the roofs or any available space and then all the sacrifices.

Throughout the week, the people were giving back to God a portion of the abundance He had given to them. In doing this, they were acknowledging the sovereignty of God—that all is His. During the time when a temple stood in Jerusalem, this week was one of the most important of the Jewish holidays. It was during the Feast of Tabernacles that the original Temple, built by King Solomon, was dedicated. The completion and dedication of the Temple is recorded in 2 Chronicles 5-7 (cf 1 Kings 8).

Take a few minutes to read through 2 Chronicles 5-7 and see how King Solomon celebrated the first day of this feast, then answer the following questions.

How is the Feast of Tabernacles referenced in 2 Chronicles 5:3?

_____

_____

_____

What praise was sung by the Levitical singers (2 Chron. 5:13)?

_____

_____

_____

What happened in "the house of the Lord" after the singing (2 Chron. 5:13b-14)?

_____

_____

_____

On the first day of the feast, King Solomon offered up 22,000 oxen and 120,000 sheep. Seriously, I cannot even image it. Just the blood that was shed would have been a sight (and the smell), one which was a reminder to the people that death is necessary for redemption. Even during a joyous feast such as this the reminder is there of what is required to come before a holy God.

But on this day hundreds of years after the instructions for the Feast of Tabernacles were given by God to Moses, this new generation of people got to see what their ancestors had experienced with the original Tabernacle. On this day, He showed His approval of the people's work on His Temple and of their praise by filling the building with His glory. He so consumed the place that no one could enter and how amazing that must have been for those present that day. Their God had given His approval and chosen to dwell in their midst within the house they offered to Him. That is one of the things the Feast of Tabernacles celebrates, that Holy God dwelt in the midst of an unholy people providing and protecting them in the wilderness wanderings. Even wandering that was due to the sin of the people against God. The feast, like this day in Israel's history, celebrates God's love, unmerited and enduring.

At this feast, King Solomon offered up a prayer to God for the people and himself. In 2 Chronicles 6, Solomon is described as getting down on his knees in front of all the people and raising his hands toward heaven when he prayed.

What is the first thing Solomon states in his prayer (6:14-15)?

_____

_____

_____

_____

_____

_____

_____

_____

In his prayer, Solomon first addresses that God is the only God in heaven and on earth, He is faithful to keep His promises, and He shows enduring love to those *who walk before Him with all their heart*. Next, the king reminds God of His promise to Solomon's father to always have a descendant of David's on the throne of Israel. But he notes that there is a condition to David's descendants, which was they would walk in the law of the Lord as David had done before God. His prayer continues by asking the Lord to hear the cries and concerns of the people concerning whatever might come upon them in the future, such as famine, pestilence, war, sickness, etc.

This prayer showed a couple of things about King Solomon. One, he knew who the God of Israel was and what He expected of not only the people but also the king. He knew that all Israel had or needed would come from the Lord, He was their protector, healer and provider in all things. That was really another of the reasons for the Feast of Tabernacles, to celebrate the provisions of God. So it was very fitting that the Temple built for Him be dedicated at this feast.

After his prayer, the Lord appeared to the king and made him a promise.

2 Chronicles 7:12b-22 "I have heard your prayer and have chosen this place for myself as a house of sacrifice. When I shut up the heavens so that there is no rain, or command the locust to devour the land, or send pestilence among my people, if my people who are called by my name humble themselves, and pray and seek my face and turn from their wicked ways, then I will hear from heaven and will forgive their sin and heal their land. Now my eyes will be open and my ears attentive to the prayer that is made in this place. For now I have chosen and consecrated this house that my name may be there forever. My eyes and my heart will be there for all time. And as for you, if you will walk before me as David your father walked, doing according to all that I have commanded you and keeping my statutes and my rules, then I will establish your royal throne, as I covenanted with David your father, saying 'You shall not lack a man to rule Israel.' But if you turn aside and forsake my statutes and my commandments that I have set before you, and go and serve other gods and worship them, then I will pluck you up from my land that I have given you, and this house that I have consecrated for my name, I will cast out of my sight, and I will make it a proverb and a byword among all peoples. And at this house, which was exalted, everyone passing by will be

astonished and say 'Why has the LORD done thus to this land and to this house?'
Then they will say, 'Because they abandoned the LORD, the God of their fathers who
brought them out of the land of Egypt and laid hold on other gods and worshiped them
and served them. Therefore he has brought all this disaster on them.'"

This was not an unconditional promise like many of God's covenants. He gave conditions
to both the people of Israel and to King Solomon personally.

What condition was given to the people (7:14)?

_____

_____

_____

And what condition was given to the king (7:17)?

_____

_____

_____

The people were to humble themselves before God, pray to Him, seek after Him and turn
away from wickedness. In reality, only by pursuing the first three can we hope to do the
fourth. As for the king, he was to walk before God as his father, David, which meant he also
would live by the Lord's commands and not fall into idolatry. Of course, the commands to
the people included the king. But if they went against His commandments and committed
idolatry the Lord would remove them from the land and cast away the temple. The account
in 1 Kings states He would make the temple "a heap of ruins," which He did in 586 B.C.
(1 Kings 9:8). The Lord's actions would be a testimony to the nations, who would know the
reason He did it was because Israel had abandoned Him. All that the Lord instructed them
to do pointed them to a relationship with Him, which is what He has desired since creation.

But why on a day of such great celebration would God give the King such a severe warning?
For the very same reason God established the annual feasts, to remind Israel of His love and
of whom they worshiped. He knew they were going to do exactly what He warned not to
do. That has to be so frustrating knowing the consequences would not stop them because
they became a people who were comfortable. Remember that during Solomon's reign in
Israel's history, they were a strong nation of great wealth who did not anticipate that their
king would marry foreign princesses and allow idol worship to occur in their land, but he
did. They did not expect that they, the same people who had been on their faces in worship
of Jehovah God, would participate in the worship of foreign gods, but they did. God knew
all this and He loved them enough to warn them.

In the years of Solomon's temple, the people would come joyfully from all over the Promised
Land to spend a week in worship of the One True God. Those traveling may have had
a more heightened excitement since they did not have the privilege of worshiping every

Sabbath at the Temple. We have seen throughout this study that the sacrificial system was central to Israel's worship. I think we need to remember that it is also central to our worship. Unless we understand the point of sacrifice, we will not grasp the full meaning of Christ's death on the cross. We need to understand that this feast celebrated something else crucial to Israel but also to Christians today. This feast celebrated the fact that God had dwelt in the midst of His people. Christians should celebrate the fact that Christ now dwells within individual believers and our response to that is our praise and worship.

The Feast of Tabernacles was a seven day worship celebration filled with joy. That is exactly what worship is, a privilege that should be entered into with joy. How excited were we to come together this week for corporate worship? It is so important that we realize worship is a privilege we should enter into with joy and gratitude focused on Christ Jesus. My prayer is that we glean this truth from our study of the feasts and live it out.

Day 3 - The Word became Flesh

I want to warn you this is going to be another really full day, so get yourself a cup of coffee and comfy chair, but hang with it. Yesterday, we looked at the dedication of the first temple in Jerusalem, which took place during the celebration of the Feast of Tabernacles. God made His presence known to Solomon in the same way He had to Moses almost five hundred years earlier at the completion of the Tabernacle. Until Solomon's Temple, God had dwelt in the midst of His people in a tent, which allowed Him to move with them in the wilderness and Promised Land. Then a beautiful building was erected in God's honor in the city of Jerusalem.

> **Do you remember how God made it known that**
> **He approved of the original Temple?**

_____

_____

_____

God filled the building with His glory like a cloud in such a way that no one could stand inside. The temple provided what the people thought would be a more permanent dwelling place for God. Solomon described it as a place for God *to dwell in forever* (2 Chron 6:2b). But, of course, He would not dwell in that or any earthly temple forever. The king and the people did not honor God's covenant but, instead, did exactly what God warned them against, they followed after foreign, pagan gods. So the Lord's glory eventually departed from the Temple and, as promised by God, the building was *cast out of His sight* when it was destroyed by the Babylonians.

The glory of God did not return to Jerusalem until hundreds of years after the Temple's destruction but not in the way the people expected. The Lord's glory returned to Herod's temple, which was the building built by the returned Jewish exiles and expanded by Herod, but not in a cloud, it was with a baby. The glory of God entered the Temple in the arms of Mary and Joseph (see Luke 2:25-32) and each time Jesus walked through the doors during His earthly life.

John 1:1-5, 14 "In the beginning was the Word, and the Word was with God, and the Word was God. He was in the beginning with God. All things were made through him, and without him was not any thing made that was made. In him was life, and the life was the light of men. The light shines in the darkness, and the darkness has not overcome it . . . And the Word became flesh and dwelt among us, and we have seen his glory, glory as of the only Son from the Father, full of grace and truth.

Write down everything the above passage teaches concerning the Word.

_____

_____

_____

The apostle John tells us that the Word was God and the Word became flesh, which means God became flesh, or human. The Word in this passage is Jesus. And so if God became human, then Jesus is God. Jesus is God who took on human flesh and lived among mankind. The gospel writer states that when anyone looked on Him, they saw the Lord's glory. The glory of God returned to Israel when the incarnate Word took up residence on earth.

The apostle John writes that the Word (Jesus) *dwelt among us*. The word *dwelt* in the Greek is 'skenoo'[52] which means *to set up one's tent* or *dwell in a tent*. I love the way the ESV Study Bible notes explain this word. "Dwelt among us means more literally 'pitched his tent,' an allusion to God's dwelling among the Israelites in the tabernacle. In the past, God had manifested his presence among his people in the tabernacle and the temple. Now God takes up residence among his people in the incarnate Word, Jesus Christ"[53] Jesus' coming is the fulfillment of the Feast of Tabernacles, which is a picture of God dwelling in the midst of mankind. John Piper explains that "God came to live in a tent so we can watch him more closely, God wants to be seen and known in his Son."[54]

The Lord brought the people of Israel out of Egypt to dwell among them and be their God. His tabernacle, or tent, was always set up right in the middle of camp. That tabernacle in the midst of the tribes of Israel was a picture of Christ coming to live among mankind and provide the way to relationship with the Father. Even the name announced for Jesus by the angels, Emmanuel, speaks to this in its meaning, *God with us*. Jesus Christ *tabernacled* with His people just as the Father had in the wilderness, but sadly most of the people did not know the glory of God was among them again.

As I am writing this week's study we have just finished Thanksgiving and are embarking on the Christmas season. We started today putting up some of our decorations, the first of which was one of our nativity scenes. This study is such a reminder to me of all my God has done for me and how amazing it is that He chose to leave heaven to live here. Our Lord came and set up His tent among us as a babe with nothing but a food trough and a stable for a home. Yet, the Father made sure His coming was announced with greater fanfare than the wealthiest earthly king. Angels sang His praises and announced to shepherds in a field that God had come to be with us and set up His tent smack in the middle where all could see and come near. It was because of God's grace that He chose to dwell in the center of Israel. The apostle John writes that it is from Jesus that we receive that grace, for He is *full of grace and truth* (1:14b).

Jesus Christ's coming to live among us is the fulfillment of the Feast of Tabernacles. By living in booths, or tents, the people were remembering how their ancestors had lived in tents for forty years in the wilderness before entering the Promised Land, how God had lived and walked with their ancestors, all the while providing and protecting them, and were looking forward to the promise of God when Jesus would come in the flesh to *provide* for all the world salvation.

The Feast of Tabernacles was observed in Jesus' time and Scripture records His presence in Jerusalem for the feast during His ministry years. He observed all of the feasts commanded in the Law. But there were actually additions to the feast sometime before Jesus' era. These additions are not instructed in Scripture, however, made for excellent teaching moments. I want us to look at one of those teaching moments in the remainder of today's study.

Please read John 7 and answer the following questions.

Which feast was being celebrated (7:2)?_____

Who attended the feast (7:10)? _____

Where was Jesus mid-week (7:14)? _____

What were the people seeking to do concerning Jesus (7:19, 30, 32)?

_____

The feast John references in this chapter is the Feast of Booths (7:2), also known as the Feast of Tabernacles. And, in the middle of the week, Jesus was teaching in the temple (7:14). That was no surprise as he often was found teaching in the temple. On the last day of the feast, John says Jesus "stood up and cried out 'If anyone thirsts, let him come to me and drink'" (7:37). Remember the eighth day was to be observed as a holy assembly, or Sabbath, and not only marked the end of this feast week, it also marked the end of Israel's harvest year. Certainly they should have been focused on thanking God for His provision for that season and year; and looking to His provision for the coming year as well.

According to historians, the Jews added a ritual to the Old Testament instructions given for the Feast of Tabernacles, one which focused on their indebtedness and gratitude to God. Many believe a water drawing ceremony was added to the feast on each morning of the week, although there are differing opinions as to why it was added. Some say it was in honor of God giving the rain for their crops. Still others think it was added as a memorial to the Lord's miracle of water brought from a rock for Moses (Exodus 17:1-7).

The water-drawing ceremony was added to the Feast of Tabernacles to remember God's provision in the wilderness, to thank Him for the rains that provided their harvest, and for His provision of rain in the future. Israel understood rain to be a sign that God was blessing His people and drought as a sign of His judgment (see Deuteronomy 11:13-17). Remember, the Feast of Tabernacles was the last of the annual feasts and fell at the time of the final harvest. The people would be praying for the harvests of the coming year.

The water ceremony occurred at dawn each morning of the feast with a procession of priests and musicians leading the people to the Pool of Siloam, which was located at the southern edge of Jerusalem. All were led by the ornately adorned High Priest, who would carry a golden pitcher to be filled with water, and then he would take it back to the Temple grounds. Once back at the Temple, musicians would sound the trumpets then the priests and people would shout "With joy you will draw water from the wells of salvation" (Isaiah 12:3). The High Priest would then walk up the ramp of the outer altar where there were two basins. He would pour the water from the pitcher into one basin while wine as a drink offering to the Lord was poured in the second basin. After this, the Levitical choir would sing from the Hallel, or Psalms 113-118. Finally, the people would join in with "Save us, we pray, O Lord! O Lord, we pray, give us success!" (Psalm 118:25).[55]

Take a few minutes and read through Psalm 118.

David Brickner notes the Hallel "set the tone for the entire celebration as it was chanted at the Feast of Tabernacles. Expressing unfettered joy, it looked forward to the great deliverance when God would come and tabernacle with His people."[56]

What did Jesus announce to the people on the last day of the Feast of Tabernacles (John 7:37-38)?

_____

_____

_____

John 7:37-39 "On the last day of the feast, the great day, Jesus stood up and cried out, 'If anyone thirsts, let him come to me and drink. Whoever believes in me, as the Scripture has said, 'Out of his heart will flow rivers of living water.' Now this he said about the Spirit, whom those who believed in him were to receive, for as yet the Spirit had not been given, because Jesus was not yet glorified."

What better setting for Jesus to announce to the Jews that their long awaited salvation was at hand? It was during this ceremony that Jesus cried out that He is the *living water* that could be theirs forever. Of course, for someone to come to Jesus and drink means they believe in Him and desire a personal relationship with Him. The trumpets were being blown and the people were crying out in praise the words of the Lord, when the Lord Himself shouts to them that salvation is right there in front of them.

Isaiah 12:3-6 "With joy you will draw water from the wells of salvation. And you will say in that day: Give thanks to the Lord, call upon his name, make known his deeds among the peoples, proclaim that his name is exalted. Sing praises to the Lord, for he has done gloriously; let this be made known in all the earth. Shout, and sing for joy, O inhabitant of Zion, for great in your midst is the Holy One of Israel."

On each day of this feast the water-drawing ceremony occurred and it is believed the priests would sing from the above passage. Read over the words the prophet Isaiah penned more than seven hundred years before Jesus' day and think about how they perfectly relate to what the Lord was announcing to Israel.

The apostle John explained living water to be a reference to the Holy Spirit (John 7:39), who had not been given at that point, but was given after Jesus' ascension on the day of Pentecost (or Feast of Weeks). Of course, we know the Spirit had been at work because He is mentioned as early as creation. Various people throughout Scripture are said to have been filled with the Spirit, such as Saul, David and John the Baptist. Jesus is speaking of the indwelling of the Spirit that would be given to every believer permanently with His new covenant. For this, one must come to believing faith in the Son and, on the last day of that feast, we are told some did believe but many did not. Likewise, today the gospel divides with some believing and others ignoring, even hating it.

Throughout the week of the Feast of Tabernacles, the thoughts of the people would be focused on God's provision and salvation. Though the water-drawing ceremony was not commanded in Scripture with the instructions given for the feast, it was still used by Jesus as a means of teaching about Himself and the gift of salvation. It is another example to me of the lengths God will go to in order to draw His people to Him. This is how much He loves and cares about us.

All of Scripture from Genesis to Revelation is about the one sent to *tabernacle* in the midst of mankind and provide the means for an eternal relationship with God, Jesus Christ. The Feast of Tabernacles was a week when all of Israel remembered how Jehovah God had been present with them in the wilderness and gifted them with the land of promise. It was also a time when they looked to Him for their salvation. And this feast was a foreshadowing of Christ's coming and living among us, ultimately of believers living forever with Him.

I don't really want to stop today but there is still one day in this study. Tomorrow we will finish our look at the Feast of Tabernacles. Is anyone thinking about hanging out in a tent in your backyard?

Day 4 - All Nations will Worship the King

The Feast of Tabernacles began on Tishri 15, just five days after the most holy day of the Jewish year, the Day of Atonement. What a drastic transition from a very solemn day to a very joyous week, a week referred to in Jewish literature as the *Season of our Rejoicing*. But it seems quite reasonable to me that joy should follow the forgiveness received on the Day of Atonement. The Feast of Tabernacles was a joy-filled week celebrating the provision of God through the harvest, remembering God's provision and protection in the wilderness when He dwelt with His people, and gratitude for His provision of rain.

The prophet Zechariah wrote that the nations would celebrate the Feast of Tabernacles.

Zechariah 14:16-19 "Then everyone who survives of all the nations that have come against Jerusalem shall go up year after year to worship the King, the Lord of hosts, and to keep the Feast of Booths. And if any of the families of the earth do not go up to Jerusalem to worship the King, the Lord of hosts, there will be no rain on them. And if the family of Egypt does not go up and present themselves, then on them there shall be no rain, there shall be the plague with which the Lord afflicts the nations that do not go up to keep the Feast of Booths. This shall be the punishment to Egypt and the punishment to all the nations that do not go up to keep the Feast of Booths."

This chapter begins with an invasion of Jerusalem. Many believe Zechariah is speaking of events that will occur when the Lord returns. The chapter begins with the phrase 'a day is coming for the Lord' which could mean the same thing as "the day of the Lord." The problem is Zechariah is not an easy read for anyone. Martin Luther actually wrote two commentaries on this book. In the first, he stopped after the thirteenth chapter, completely skipping fourteen. His second commentary, though it did include chapter fourteen, had little on the chapter and even admitted that he was not sure what the prophet was saying.

On the other hand, John Calvin did have an opinion of what Zechariah meant in this chapter. He believed Zechariah was speaking of Israel after the Babylonian captivity and not speaking of the end times. Other commentators do believe he was writing about the end times. I cannot absolutely say what time frame the prophet is writing about, but I will say I do not know of any past happenings that match up with Zechariah's writing.

The safest thing is to read the prophet's writing in a *normal, straightforward fashion* unless his writing notes otherwise. The prophet Zechariah may make a good point for considering this to be speaking of end times. Zechariah writes ". . . there shall never again be a decree of utter destruction. Jerusalem shall dwell in security" (Zech 14:11). I don't know that Jerusalem has *dwelt in security* since Solomon's time, so this would lead one to believe he is writing about the future. But for our study we want to focus on the Feasts of the Lord, particularly the Feast of Tabernacles. So we will look at this passage in Zechariah in respect to the feast.

Before we go any further, please read Zechariah 14 and then answer the following:

Who fights for Israel (14:3)? _____

What will happen to the Mount of Olives (14:4)?_____

On the day described by Zechariah, who will rule over the earth (14:9)?

_____

What will those who survive the battle do annually (14:16)?

_____

What would be the judgment if any families do not go to Jerusalem to worship (14:17)? _____

At the beginning of this chapter, Jerusalem is described as under attack by all the nations, but the Lord returns to fight the battle for her, just as He so often did in the Old Testament. The prophet describes the Lord returning to the Mount of Olives, which he states will split when the Lord steps down on it. The Mount of Olives is where the Lord ascended into heaven two thousand years ago. And with His return, He will assume His position of *king over all the earth*. Don't you just want to shout Hallelujah?

According to the prophet, all who survive the battle will worship at the Feast of Booths. In verse 16, Zechariah writes of people from *all the nations* traveling to Jerusalem to *worship the King, the Lord of Hosts* and participate in *the Feast of Booths*. What an amazing sight that will be when masses of Jews and Gentiles worship the Lord Jesus in Jerusalem. The prophet describes these worshipers as everyone who *survives of all the nations that have come against Jerusalem* (14:16). Those who at one time will be against Jerusalem will have a change of heart and worship the Lord there. And they will celebrate the last of the Lord's annual feasts, the Feast of Tabernacles. Gentiles included in this celebration should not be a surprise for back in Deuteronomy 16, Gentiles were included.

"You shall keep the Feast of Booths seven days, when you have gathered in the produce from your threshing floor and your winepress. You shall rejoice in your feast (Tabernacles), you and your son and your daughter, your male servant and your female servant, the Levite, the sojourner, the fatherless, and the widow who are within your towns. For seven days you shall keep the feast to the Lord your God at the place that the Lord will choose, because the Lord your God will bless you in all your produce and in all the work of your hands, so that you will be altogether joyful" (Deuteronomy 16:13-15).

A *sojourner* is a stranger or foreigner to Israel. God's desire has always been for the world to know Him, not just Israel. His promise to Abraham was that "in you [Abraham] all the families of the earth shall be blessed" (Genesis 12:3). This promise was repeated to Isaac and Jacob (Genesis 26:4; 28:14). Any foreigner in Israel at the time of the feast could be included in the celebration. The feast was to be held at the place that the Lord would choose, His choice later being Jerusalem. According to Zechariah, all the nations will come together *year after year* to the *place of the Lord's choosing* for worship of the King, the Lord of Hosts. The people who at one time hate and desire to destroy Jerusalem will one day come to the city to worship Christ. If they don't, the Lord will withhold the rain from them, for He is the God of the harvest, Creator of the universe and He can withhold rain if He sees it as right to do.

This also shows that these foreigners will be treated just as the Lord stated concerning Israel. Yesterday we looked at a passage in Deuteronomy 11 when the Lord warned Israel that if they did not live in obedience to His commands, He would withhold the rain. The same is held true in Zechariah for the other nations. Now I have already said I don't know what time frame Zechariah is writing about in this passage and some make valid points for it being end times. But I would be really negligent if I did not point out that this issue sort of points to it not being end times that the prophet is writing about because once Christ establishes His kingdom, rain won't be an issue. Now do you see Luther's point of not knowing for sure what the prophet was saying?

But why will the nations celebrate the Feast of Tabernacles? This is one of the feasts that honors the Lord for His provision and for dwelling among His people in the wilderness.

God desires to live among us and to have a relationship with us, all of us (even Gentiles). I believe this feast is the perfect picture of that truth. Zechariah states that *all the nations* will one day come together to worship the true King. Christ came to this earth in human form and dwelt, or *tabernacled*, among us. He dwells today with anyone who is a true believer and worshiper now through His Spirit that He sent to us. The apostle John wrote ". . . The kingdom of the world has become the kingdom of our Lord and of his Christ, and he shall reign forever and ever" (Revelation 11:15b). I don't know if that is what the prophet Zechariah had in mind when he penned his book. But I do know that Christ desires that our lives be lived out as citizens of that kingdom now. We are to live our lives according to His teaching and example. And we may not build booths once a year to celebrate the Feast of Tabernacles, but we can respond with joy to Christ's gift of salvation by living our lives according to His gospel with love for our King. Christians live in this world but we are to live as citizens of heaven.

***Colossians 3:1-4** "If then you have been raised with Christ, seek the things that are above, where Christ is, seated at the right hand of God. Set your minds on things that are above, not on things that are on earth. For you have died, and your life is hidden with Christ in God. When Christ who is your life appears, then you also will appear with him in glory."*

In this passage, the apostle Paul states that we are to seek the things of heaven and set our minds on them. This requires a deliberate or intentional action on our part. As citizens of Christ's heaven, believers are to desire and determine to live according to His instructions, not follow the ways of the world around us. But we need to ask ourselves 'Is Christ my life?' 'Do I live like He is my life?' If He is our very life, then we will want to spend time with Him in prayer and study His Word in order to better understand His teaching.

The Feast of Tabernacles was an annual celebration of God dwelling among His people during their wilderness wanderings. It was also a picture of the coming of God's Son who would dwell among His people. And, since His ascension, the Lord Jesus dwells (or tabernacles) within every believer, which is reason for joy and celebration every day, not just once a year. Until we see Christ physically, we need to live everyday of our lives in such a way that the world can see Him *tabernacling* here within His people.

Our study of the Lord's feasts has come to a close. The feasts of the Lord were established so that God's people would remember His past deeds, recognize His provision, and rejoice in His presence. God's desire has always been for a relationship with us, both Jew and Gentile. These feasts were a means of reminding Israel of their God. And each feast points to the coming of Jesus Christ and His provision of salvation for all who believe. My hope and desire is that each person who goes through this study will finish it with a greater love for God's Word and desire to grow in their relationship with Jesus Christ. My prayer for each one of you is from Paul's letter to the Colossians.

***Colossians 3:15-17** "And let the peace of Christ rule in your hearts, to which indeed you were called in one body. And be thankful. Let the word of Christ dwell in you richly, teaching and admonishing one another in all wisdom, singing psalms and hymns and spiritual songs, with thankfulness in your hearts to God. And whatever you do, in word or deed, do everything in the name of the Lord Jesus, giving thanks to God the Father through him."*

Endnotes

1. David Brickner, <u>Christ in the Feast of Tabernacles</u>. Moody Publishers, Chicago, Il., 2006, page 9.

2. Spiros Zodhiates, Editor. <u>Hebrew-Greek Key Word Study Bible</u>. AMB Publishers, Chattanoogo, TN, 1977, page 1781.

3. Ibid., page 1770.

4. Douglas K. Stuart. <u>The New American Commentary-Exodus</u>. Broadman and Holman Publishers, Nashville, TN, 2006, page 457.

5. <u>ESV Study Bible</u>. English Standard Version. Crossway Bibles, Wheaton, Il,. 2008, page 196.

6. Kevin Howard and Marvin Rosenthal. <u>The Feasts of the Lord</u>. Thomas Nelson, Inc., Nashville, TN, 1997, page 51.

7. Douglas K. Stuart. <u>The New American Commentary-Exodus</u>. Broadman and Holman Publishers, Nashville, TN, 2006, page 272.

8. John MacArthur. <u>The MacArthur Bible Commentary</u>. Nelson Reference and Electronic, Nashville, TN, 2005, page 99.

9. John F. Walvoord and Roy B. Zuck. <u>The Bible Knowledge Commentary-Old Testament</u>. Cook Communications Ministries, Colorado Springs, Colorado, 2004, page 126.

10. John Sailhamer. <u>The Pentateuch as Narrative</u>. Zondervan Publishing House, Grand Rapids, Michigan, 1992, page 262.

11. <u>ESV Study Bible</u>. English Standard Version. Crossway Bibles, Wheaton, Il,. 2008, page 2367.

12. Ceil and Moishe Rosen. <u>Christ in the Passover</u>. Moody Publishers, Chicago, Il., 2006, page 37.

13. Craig A. Evans. <u>The Bible Knowledge Background Commentary-Matthew-Luke</u>. Cook Communication Ministries, Colorado Springs, Colorado, 2003, page 477.

14. John Phillips. <u>Exploring 1 Corinthians</u>. Kregel Publications, Grand Rapids, MI, 2002, page 252.

15. <u>ESV Study Bible</u>. English Standard Version. Crossway Bibles, Wheaton, Il,. 2008, page 1881.

16. John Sailhamer. <u>The Pentateuch as Narrative</u>. Zondervan Publishing House, Grand Rapids, Michigan, 1992, page 152.

17. Douglas K. Stuart. <u>The New American Commentary-Exodus</u>. Broadman and Holman Publishers, Nashville, TN, 2006, page 285.

18. <u>Holman Quicksource Bible Dictionary</u>. Holman Bible Publishers, Holman Reference, Nashville, TN, 2005, page 278.

19. Ibid.

20. Strong's Greek and Hebrew Dictionary (Online). <u>Http://bible.lifeway.com/crossmain.asp</u> Strong's Hebrew # 2556.

21. Douglas K. Stuart. <u>The New American Commentary-Exodus</u>. Broadman and Holman Publishers, Nashville, TN, 2006, pages 282-283.

22. John MacArthur. <u>The MacArthur Bible Commentary</u>. Thomas Nelson, Inc., Nashville, TN, 2005, page 1573.

23. C. H. Spurgeon. <u>Christ in the Old Testament</u>. AMB Publishers, Chattanooga, TN, 1994, pages 238-239.

24. Kevin Howard and Marvin Rosenthal. <u>The Feasts of the Lord</u>. Thomas Nelson, Inc., Nashville, TN, 1997, page 76 (Antiquities of the Jews 3.10.5).

25. Ibid., page 77.

26. <u>Holman Quicksource Bible Dictionary</u>. Holman Bible Publishers, Holman Reference, Nashville, TN, 2005, page 68.

27. Frank E. Gaebelein, General Editor. <u>The Expositor's Bible Commentary-Volume 2</u>. Zondervan, Grand Rapids, MI, 1990, page 383.

28. Kevin Howard and Marvin Rosenthal. <u>The Feasts of the Lord</u>. Thomas Nelson, Inc., Nashville, TN, 1997, page 84.

29. Ibid., page 86.

30. <u>ESV Study Bible</u>. English Standard Version. Crossway Bibles, Wheaton, Il,. 2008, page 2392.

31. Kevin Howard and Marvin Rosenthal. <u>The Feasts of the Lord</u>. Thomas Nelson, Inc., Nashville, TN, 1997, page 89.

32. <u>ESV Study Bible</u>. English Standard Version. Crossway Bibles, Wheaton, Il,. 2008, page 219.

33. David Brickner and Rich Robinson. <u>Christ in the Feast of Pentecost</u>. Moody Publishers, Chicago, Il., 2008, page 46.

34. David Brickner and Rich Robinson. <u>Christ in the Feast of Pentecost</u>. Moody Publishers, Chicago, Il., 2008, page 49.

35. Kevin Howard and Marvin Rosenthal. <u>The Feasts of the Lord</u>. Thomas Nelson, Inc., Nashville, TN, 1997, page 95.

36. Ibid., page 97.

37. Ibid., page 97.

38. Norman L. Geisler. <u>A Popular Survey of the Old Testament</u>. Baker Book House, Grand Rapids, MI., 1977, page 104.

39. John B. Polhill. <u>The New American Commentary-Acts</u>. Broadman Press, Nashville, TN, 1992, page 98.

40. John F. Walvoord and Roy B. Zuck. <u>The Bible Knowledge Commentary</u>. Cook Communications Ministries, Colorado Springs, CO, 2004, page 225.

41. Strong's Greek and Hebrew Dictionary (Online). <u>Http://bible.lifeway.com/ crossmain.asp</u> Strong's Hebrew # 6942.

42. Joshua Moss. "Hearing the Sound of the Shofar." <u>Http://JewsforJesus.org/ publications/newsletter/1993 09/soundshofar</u>, Jews for Jesus Newsletter 5753:11, 09/01/93.

43. Kevin Howard and Marvin Rosenthal. <u>The Feasts of the Lord</u>. Thomas Nelson, Inc., Nashville, TN, 1997, page 111.

44. Ibid.

45. Millard J. Erickson. <u>Christian Theology</u>. Baker Academic, Grand Rapids, MI, 1998, page 822.

46. <u>The ESV Study Bible</u>, English Standard Version, Crossway Bibles, Wheaton, Illinois, 2008, page 237.

47. William Whiston, translator. <u>The Works of Josephus</u>. Hendrickson Publishers, Peabody, MA, 1987, page 95.

48. C. H. Spurgeon. <u>Christ in the Old Testament</u>. AMB Publishers, Chattanooga, TN, 1994, page 393.

49. David Brickner. <u>Christ in the Feast of Tabernacles</u>. Moody Publishers, Chicago, Il., 2006, page 21.

50. Ibid., page 24.

51. R. Dennis Cole. <u>New American Commentary-Numbers</u>. Broadman and Holman Publishers, Nashville, TN, 2000, page 480.

52. Edward W. Goodrick and John R. Kohlenberger, III. <u>The Strongest NIV Exhaustive Concordance</u>, Zondervan, Grand Rapids, Michigan, 1999, #5012, p 1591.

53. <u>The ESV Study Bible</u>, English Standard Version, Crossway Bibles, Wheaton, Illinois, 2008, page 2020

54. John Piper. Sermon "The Word became Flesh" Desiring God, December 24, 1989.

55. Kevin Howard and Marvin Rosenthal. <u>The Feasts of the Lord</u>. Thomas Nelson, Inc., Nashville, TN, 1997, pages 138-139.

56. David Brickner. <u>Christ in the Feast of Tabernacles</u>. Moody Publishers, Chicago, Il, 2006, page 88.